[Creation]

Belief Matters

[Creation]

The Apple of God's Eye

Justo L. González

General Editor, William H. Willimon

Abingdon Press

Nashville

CREATION:
THE APPLE OF GOD'S EYE

Copyright © 2015 by Abingdon Press

All rights reserved.

This book is printed on acid-free paper.

Library of Congress Cataloging-in-Publication Data

Gonzalez, Justo L.
  Creation : the apple of God's eye / Justo L. Gonzalez.—First [edition].
    pages cm.—(Belief matters ; 4)
  Includes bibliographical references.
    ISBN 978-1-4267-8595-5 (binding: pbk.)   1. Creation—Religious aspects—Christianity. I. Title.
  BT695.G66 2015
  231.7'65—dc23

                                                                          2015016259

15 16 17 18 19 20 21 22 23 24—10 9 8 7 6 5 4 3 2 1
MANUFACTURED IN THE UNITED STATES OF AMERICA

To Juanita
the apple of my eye
Dad

Contents

Editor's Introduction

What do you see when you look out your window? While others may see "nature," or "the cosmos," Christians believe we see "creation." That there is something rather than nothing, that the world we inhabit is not only useful but often beautiful, that even though we have learned much through a couple of centuries of scientific investigation of the world we still are able to stand in awe before the majesty and mystery of the world within and without us—all this is testimony to the power of our belief in the world as a creation of God.

Now, more than ever, as we honestly confront the sad results of our poor stewardship of creation, as we attempt to take responsibility as coworkers with the Creator in our defense of God's handwork, as we try to make sense of ourselves and the world around us, we, as Christians, need to think together about the significance of our conviction that the world didn't just occur; the world is creation. The world is not a place to be exploited; the world is for us sacred responsibility, tangible, visible evidence of the sort of God whose first, generative word is addressed, not to us, but to the "formless void" (Gen 1:2

NRSV): God's joyful, creative command, "Let there be light" (v. 3).

Justo González, a lifelong teacher of the history and doctrine of the church, has written a book that amply demonstrates the practical implications of—and the sheer joy of believing—the truth that we live in creation. Belief Matters is a series that encourages the best minds in the church to share with their fellow Christians why our core beliefs matter. Dr. González, in this book on creation, has taken up the challenge of communicating the importance of orthodox Christian doctrine in an exuberant, joyful hymn to the continuing God who is not only savior, redeemer, but also a relentless, unceasing Creator.

Strikingly, Dr. González has not simply written an explication of correct Christian doctrine; he has written a story about the love that creates something out of nothing, beauty out of chaos, and generates life out of death, love that moves the sun, the moon, and stars. What God did at creation, what God continues to do in us and in the world now, fresh every morning, God does out of love. Down deep, at the heart of it all is more than a set of natural laws or chemical equations. At the heart of things is a God who is not only sovereign but also lovingly creative. Therein is our hope and the world's hope as well.

—Will Willimon

What Do We Mean by *Creation*?

What do we mean by *creation*? Suppose that there is a famous fashion designer by the name of *Armand*, and a sign at a high-end fashion store reads, "Creations by Armand." We are told that a student's paper shows "great creativity." Some are accused of "creative bookkeeping." And there is even a publication called *Creative Loafing*. So before we turn to matters of faith and doctrine, it may be well to examine what the very notion of "creation" means in everyday life.

When the fashion store advertises that it is selling creations by Armand, it is referring not so much to the act of creating as to the gown it wishes to sell. So they tell prospective buyers that the gown is a "creation." In a sense every gown is somebody's creation. But the store would never put up a sign, "Creations by John Doe." What makes this particular gown more valuable is not just the gown itself, but the fact that it was created by Armand. The store calls this gown a "creation" not just because somebody made it but because it was Armand who made it. The very name of Armand gives particular value to his creation. Thus, we value the creation (the dress) because we value the creator (Armand).

Yet the opposite is also true. Were we to look at an entire collection of Armand's gowns, we would be able tell much about Armand himself, particularly about his taste and his values. So while Armand defines and gives value to his creation, the gown itself is also a reflection of Armand. In this case, we come to know the creator (Armand) through his creation (his dresses). In brief, what makes a "creation" significant is both the creation itself—in this case, the gown—and the creator—in this case, Armand.

Although one could stretch the word to mean anything that anyone makes, we normally reserve the title of *creation* for something that has other characteristics beyond the mere fact of being made.

For one, we expect a "creation" to be unique. Were Armand to mass-produce his gowns and sell thousands of them, the store would no longer call them "creations." Whoever invented the cookie cutter was probably a creative person, and therefore that first cookie-cutter was a creation. But now the very reference to a cookie-cutter is practically the exact opposite of creativity.

Second, a creation is something that the mind conceives and then brings into existence. A student is "creative" because in her mind she connects things in ways others have not done and then gives flesh to those thoughts in a paper. In this sense, a clear example of unique creativity is a composer who hears the music in his head and then composes a symphony. Think of the creativity of Beethoven, who could continue composing what he heard in his head even after his ears were no longer able to hear it!

Third, a creation has a purpose. Every doodle is unique and, no matter how briefly, every line was in the mind of the doodler before being on paper. But one would hardly call a doodle a creation. (Certainly not the doodles I produce while listening to a boring lecture!) Armand's gowns are creations because he has conceived and then produced them with a purpose, with a vision, as an attempt to express something, because even before he drew its outline he not only could see it on the body of a model but there was also a statement he wished to make by it.

Fourth, a creation, once produced, has a life of its own. The gown that Armand created will be worn at a gala somewhere. In creating the gown, Armand has produced something that others will wear, and Armand's will and message, though still in the gown, may well be either reinforced or obscured when it is worn at a ball. He may have wished for it to be a statement on elegance, and it may be worn shabbily. Or it may be worn by a woman of refinement, who thus reinforces his statement. The tune for the song "Simple Gifts," created as an expression of the joy of a simple life, has now become the background music for advertising a luxury car. It is still a joyful song. But it is no longer a praise of simplicity!

As we shall see in the chapters that follow, when we speak of "creation" in the context of faith, we mean all these things: creation's greatest value is the stamp of its Creator on it (like Armand's label on a dress); creation reflects and expresses the nature of its Creator; it is unique; it comes from the mind of the Creator; it has a purpose; and it has a life of its own.

Creation bears the stamp of the Creator, expresses the nature of the Creator, and comes from the mind of the Creator.

But then the notion of creativity goes beyond that, as may be seen in phrases such as "creative bookkeeping" and "creative loafing." There is a sense in which the God in whom we believe practices a sort of creative bookkeeping in dealing with our sins—a bookkeeping in which our debts are canceled by God's grace. And, surprisingly, as we shall see, God also practices a sort of creative loafing! But perhaps it is best not to get too far ahead of ourselves...

Discussion Questions

1. What is something that you have created? Do you consider yourself a creative person? Think of people whom you know who are creative. What makes them creative?

2. Share a moment when you experienced the wonder of God's creation.

3. When people talk about creation care, what does it mean to you? According to your understanding of the Bible, what are our responsibilities to care for God's creation?

4. How are people reflections of God's image? In what ways can you reflect God in your daily life?

Creation as an Act of Love

A Creation Born of Love

"God is love," says the First Epistle of John (4:8). This is at the very core of our faith and of our religious experience. We believe that God is love because we have experienced God's care and forgiveness. But there is much more to God's love than forgiveness of sins. In the very act of creation the love of God is made manifest. God does not need creation. God needs no one but God. Yet, God has created. God has taken the awful chance of creating something that is not God, something beyond God-self. We often say that God is like a parent. This is true. But we forget that a good parent's greatest leap of love is not the act of providing for a child's needs. It is not protecting it from evil. It is not even forgiving the child's shortcomings. A parent's—or a couple's—greatest act of love is in taking the risk of creating—or adopting—someone other than themselves; someone in whom they will invest their resources, their dreams, and their own lives; someone who they know at some point will disobey them and perhaps even break their hearts; someone whom they will always love, no matter what. A parent's greatest act of love is being willing to invest love in another and commit to love that other under any and all circumstances.

The greatest act of God's love is taking a risk on us.

Another! That is the first requirement of true love. When we say that we love something or someone, we mean that we truly cherish their otherness. I love a play because it comes at me from beyond myself yet touches something inside of me. When two people love one another, we tend to say that they do so because they have much in common. That is true. But they can only truly love one *another* if they are also different, if there is and always remains an indissoluble otherness. It is that otherness that begets a constant and inexhaustible newness in their relationship. A father loves his child not just because that child is "his spitting image" but also because that child is not he; the child is another. A mother loves her child not just because it is cute and cuddly but also because it is not she; the child is a different person—one who both imitates and challenges her. We may not like it when our children disobey us, but if we truly love them, we will rejoice in the fact that they can actually disobey, that they are not we, but another.

A supposed love that does not allow the beloved to be a different person, to have different thoughts and tastes, is not true love but destructive possessiveness. True love can only be vested in one who is truly another.

True love means investing in one who is truly another.

Another! That is what this loving God of ours has made in the very act of creation. God has given birth to another reality that it not God. In deciding to have a child a responsible couple decides to take a risk, to bring into the world someone who will be different from them, someone who at some point will rebel against them. Likewise, God has decided that there will be another, an entire creation at once reflecting God's nature and free to rebel against God's will. This is God's first, mysterious, inscrutable, yet wonderful act of love.

It is an act of love that not only creates another but also cherishes and respects the otherness of the created. Otherwise, it would not be true love. Paul says that love "doesn't seek its own advantage" (1 Cor 13:5)—it is not possessive, does not turn the other into a mere object for self-fulfillment. As Jewish philosopher Martin Buber put it, "Love does not cling to the *I* in such a way as to have the *Thou* only for its 'content,' its object; but love is *between I* and *Thou*. The man who does not know this, with his very being know this, does not know love."[1]

So when we speak of creation, we are first of all speaking about God, just as when we speak of a "creation by Armand" we are speaking about Armand—his imagination, his good taste, his daring. When we say that God is the Creator, we are not just trying to explain how things came into being. We are saying that the ultimate reality, that beyond which there is no other, is God, and that this God is love!

7

Creation Is Not Primarily about *How* but about *Who*

There is a common notion that creation is about origins: that it is primarily a story, or an explanation, or a myth about how all things began. Creation is certainly related to origins—and to that we shall return later. But creation is above all about relationships, about how God relates to the world, and about how we are to relate to God and to the world.

> ## What concerns us about creation is not *how* the world was made but *who* made it.

When Christianity first appeared on the scene, the Romans had conquered the entire Mediterranean world, and as people moved from their native lands to other regions the many different cultures of the area would clash, mingle, and influence one another. Even before that, Babylonian and Egyptian creation myths had widely circulated in the Near East and had resulted in a variety of combinations. Thus stories of origins abounded—some explaining why nature seems to die in winter and is reborn in spring, others explaining the origins of various constellations, and still others dealing with national and ethnic origins.

Christians—as well as Jews—objected to all of these stories. But the main reason for their objection was not that they explained the origins of the world in a way that differed from scripture on how the world was made. Actually, in the ancient

Near East, particularly in Mesopotamia, there were stories of the origins of things that were very similar to the stories in Genesis. For instance, in the Mesopotamian creation story known as *Enuma Elish*, clearly older than the Genesis stories, the order in which various elements appear is very similar to what we find in Genesis 1: First, there was a desolate and disordered waste (Gen 1:2). Then came light (Gen 1:3). Then a dome appeared, providing the space where the rest of creation would take place (Gen 1:6-7). Next the dry land was created (Gen 1:9-10), followed by the sun, the moon, and the stars (Gen 1:14-15). Finally, humans came into the scene (Gen 1:26-27), and the gods rested and celebrated their achievement (Gen 2:2-3). Then, there is the Mesopotamian *Epic of Gilgamesh*, which in many ways parallels the story of Adam and Eve in Genesis.

In spite of their obvious connection with the biblical stories, Christians and Jews did not find these Mesopotamian stories any more acceptable than the stories of the Greeks or the Egyptians. Had there been a story that agreed in every detail with the biblical tradition, but said that this was the work of several gods, that story would have been as unacceptable as any other. This was so because the main objection to all these stories had little to do with the stories themselves. What Jews and Christians found objectionable in them was that they proposed a multiplicity of gods—or at least two eternal principles, in some other stories—in constant struggle with each other. In brief, the main interest of both Jews and Christians was not *how* the world was made but *who* made it.

One Creation by One God

This Judeo-Christian insistence on the one God had far-reaching consequences. A world under the rule of many gods was one in which order would be difficult to discern. If there is a god of rain and a god of sunshine, the weather simply depends on which of these two gods happens to have the upper hand at a particular time. If nature seems to die in winter and live again in spring, this must be because there is a god of death who rules during the long dark days of winter and is then overcome by a god of life as spring breaks forth into new life. There is little point in trying to understand such a world, where everything depends on the whims, jealousies, and struggles of the gods. But if there is a single God, Creator of all that exists, there must be an order in creation—an order that somehow makes sense and, therefore, one may try to discern. It is no coincidence that it was mostly within the context of the monotheistic Abrahamic religions—Judaism, Christianity, and Islam—that scientific inquiry developed. Certainly some of this inquiry had its roots in traditionally polytheistic Greece, but this coincided with a period when Greek thinkers themselves were criticizing traditional polytheism.

Certainly, in all of these Abrahamic religions there have been tendencies opposed to such inquiry. Some of these tendencies have stemmed from an otherworldly mysticism that lays so much stress on the spiritual world that the material is undervalued or even despised. Others have been the result of a conservative literalism that seeks to use sacred scriptures as a means to control both the mind and the social order. Such tendencies have not disappeared and may still be seen in some radical Islamists as well as in some fundamentalist Christians.

But even so, the doctrine of creation tells us that the world is orderly. We may not understand many of its mysteries. Yet any such mysteries are not the result of the capriciousness of the gods but rather of the limits of the human mind or of our present knowledge.

God creates out of God's *steadfast* loving-kindness.

In the history of Christianity itself, there were long centuries in which it was thought that the best way to approach and to know God was through contemplation of the divine mysteries and by ignoring the material world as much as possible. Early in the fifth century, St. Augustine deplored the time he had spent observing the antics of a lizard when he should have been contemplating the mysteries of God. In the late eleventh century, St. Anselm was convinced that, since everything in the world is ephemeral, the only way really to prove the existence of God was by ignoring the world and looking into reason itself, in abstraction from everything else. During those centuries many in Islam took the opposite tack, with the result that the Muslim civilization of North Africa and the Near East was far more advanced than Christian Europe. Then, in the thirteenth century, there was an important change in Christian theology. A theologian and scholar known as Albert the Great was convinced that God and truth may be known by the observation of the physical world, which is God's creation, and therefore wrote on a number of subjects that scholars had theretofore despised or undervalued—including that very zoology that

Augustine would have decried. Following these lines of thought, Albert's disciple Thomas Aquinas brought about a radical shift in Christian theology, basing much of the knowledge of God in the observation of God's creatures and thus opening the way for the great explosion of science and technology in which we are still living.

Thus, even though today many would see a conflict between science and religion, or between evolution and creation, the fact is that modern science and technology were born out of the doctrine of creation—a creation brought about by a single God and therefore making some sort of sense.

It is important for us to remember this as we look at the Christian doctrine of creation. Today, when we read in the newspaper that there is a discussion about creation—often about whether or not it should be taught in schools—we immediately think that the disagreement has to do with the how: Six days or billions of years? Or, as the question is often posed: Creation or evolution? In brief, the question seems to be, *How?*

Two Stories of Creation

But the truth is that the Bible is not particularly concerned with the *how* of creation. Actually, even before the time of Jesus, Jews who studied scripture had noted that in the first chapters of Genesis there is not one but two stories of creation, and if taken literally the two are incompatible. Early Christian scholars agreed, for they too, in reading the first chapters of Genesis, found two stories that, while similar, were still quite different.

We too can easily corroborate this. If you open your Bible and read it carefully, you will note that there is a story of creation in Genesis 1:1–2:3. This story begins with the well-known words, "In the beginning when God created the heavens and the earth..." (NRSV). But then in Genesis 2:4 the story of creation seems to begin again: "This is the account of the heavens and the earth when they were created. On the day that the Lord God made earth and sky..." If you then compare the previous story with the one that follows, you will find stark differences—as well as common themes, to which we shall return. This first story is organized in seven days. The second makes no mention of any such days. Then the order of events is different: In the first account, God made the human creature (Gen 1:26) after creating "every living creature that moves" in the waters and in the air (Gen 1:21 NRSV) and then all the animals that walk and creep on earth (Gen 1:24-25). It is only after all the rest of creation is completed that God creates the first humans, both male and female at the same time. In the second story, the order is quite different. Man—the male—is created almost at the very beginning, before plants and animals (Gen 2:7). Then God plants the garden of Eden, and there places the man, as well as all sorts of plants and the two trees—one "of life," and the other "of the knowledge of good and evil" (Gen 2:8-9). It is only after all of this has been done that God declares that "it is not good that the man should be alone" (Gen 2:18 NRSV) and sets out to make a partner for him. Then the various animals are created and brought to the man who names each of them (Gen 2:19-20). But none of these is fit company for him. It is at this point that God finally puts the man to sleep, takes a rib from him, and out of that rib makes the woman (Gen 2:21-22).

Two creation stories, four Gospels, but one God.

Believers have been aware of the differences between these two stories for a long time—Jewish believers, long before the advent of Christianity. Through the centuries, they have explained these differences in various ways. Some—such as Origen, in the early third century—even explained the apparent disparities by asserting that there are two stories of creation because there were indeed two creations—first a purely spiritual one in which sex did not exist, for humans were created "male and female," and then a physical creation in which people received bodies as well as sexual differences. In more recent times, scholars have suggested that these two stories—as well as the rest of the Pentateuch—reflect varying traditions within Israel. Although at first such scholars believed that they could readily distinguish among these traditions (listing up to four of them), the general consensus today is that the matter is much more complicated, for there is a multiplicity of sources and traditions interwoven in the entire narrative.

No matter how one explains the differences between the two creation stories in Genesis, there is no doubt that in the first chapters of Genesis there are two stories and that if these are taken as actual accounts of the process of creation they are clearly incompatible—which means that we cannot take them literally; if we did so they would be contradicting one another.

The Value of Having Two Stories

While the presence of two different creation stories in Genesis may at first puzzle us and lead us to question the validity of the Bible, upon further reflection it should not be so. Were there only one story, we could easily take it literally, memorize it, and have done with it. Actually, this is what many do when they defend "the biblical account" of creation. What they call the biblical account is usually a selection and compilation from the two stories, perhaps handed down from generation to generation, which a reading of the Bible itself would soon bring into question. Such an account simply ignores all in the Genesis stories that does not fit into it. Yet those who hold to it and defend it are convinced that it is the true and only possible account and therefore see every different account as a challenge to the Bible and to its truth. This can be very convenient, for once we know the account of creation we can easily file it away and move on to other things.

But the fact that in the first chapters of Genesis there are two stories, and that both are the word of God, means that we can never fully take possession and control of the story. Something similar happens in the New Testament, where we have not two but four different accounts of Jesus and his teachings. If we had only the Gospel of John, we could memorize it and claim that we know all there is to know about Jesus. But the very presence of four different Gospels, all attesting to the same truth, which cannot be combined into a single seamless whole, repeatedly forces us to correct and expand what we think we already know about Jesus. Having four Gospels that we cannot systematize into a single whole forces us to return to them over and over, never thinking that we possess the whole truth but always allowing God to speak to us through them. In brief, having four Gospels means that, no matter how much we study and even memorize them, they will always remain God's word to us, a word we can never master or control; God's word calls us to new insights and new dimensions of obedience.

The same is true of the two stories in Genesis. Had we only one story, we could easily memorize it, claim that we know all that we need to know about creation, and no longer need the biblical narratives. Had we only one story, we could make it *our* word, and thereby avoid the challenge of having to face *God's* word again and again—the word that is ever calling us to new insights and new forms of obedience.

When we read the Gospels we are not particularly concerned with whether it is Matthew or Luke that has the Beatitudes right. We neither discard one of them nor simply compile them into one. We use each to enrich the other as well as to force us to look more deeply into their meaning. Likewise, when we read the stories of creation in Genesis and discover that they are different, we must neither discard them nor create a compilation that solves all problems but is not true to the biblical text. Rather, we must read both of them as the word of God, and see what both tell us about creation and its meaning. Thus, throughout this book, as we deal with different issues, we shall have occasion to come back to those first chapters in Genesis and find in them much wisdom and guidance that we might otherwise miss.

On the *How*: Creation and Evolution

These days, the moment you mention the word *creation*, people think about evolution. Some say, "How can you believe in creation when science has proven that the universe is millions and millions of years old and that species evolve from

other species? Anyone who believes in creation must be ignorant and superstitious." And others say, with equal conviction,
"How can you believe in evolution when the Bible says that
God made the world in six days? Anyone who does not believe
the biblical story of creation is a disbelieving sinner, going directly to hell."

Let us look first at the "religious" side. First of all, since
there are two different stories of creation in Genesis. When
people say they defend *the* biblical account of creation what
they are defending is not really the biblical account but certain
points of it and not others. For instance, does the biblical account say that God created first everything else and finally the
first human couple, or does it say that God created first the
man, then the animals, and finally the woman?

But there is more. When we take the biblical account(s)
as an actual description of how events evolved, we lower the
authority of the Bible to that of a scientific theory. Scientific
theories are important and valuable, for it is through them
that science advances. But by their very nature all theories are
temporary. When my father studied such matters in school, he
knew that molecules were formed by atoms and that the atom
was the smallest unit of matter. Then, a generation later, we
knew that atoms could be smashed and that there were pro-
tons, electrons, and neutrons, which were the smallest possible
particles. Now we *know* that there are quite a few other particles of which I never heard while I was is school. What will
my grandchildren *know*? If we place the Bible at the level of
this sort of knowledge, we turn it into one more theory, into
another plausible explanation that is useful and valuable until
we know better.

This has happened before at other points in the history of the church and usually with dire consequences. When Copernicus argued that the earth revolved around the sun, those who defended the biblical account as scientific description felt compelled to reject his theory. After all, had not Joshua cried, "Sun, stand still at Gibeon! / And Moon, in the valley of Aijalon!" (Josh 10:12)? Today, no matter what the Bible says, most people believe that the earth revolves around the sun, and not vice versa. Thus, all that those opponents of Copernicus succeeded in doing was placing the Bible at the level of a scientific document that later discoveries would surpass—just as any genuinely scientific document or theory will eventually be surpassed or corrected.

In brief, believers do the Bible no service by turning it into a scientific account of how the world was made. The biblical doctrine of creation is not primarily about the *how* but rather about the *who* and the *for what*. It is about who stands behind creation and about the purpose of it all.

> ## The Bible is not primarily about the *how* but about the *who* and the *for what*.

If we then turn to the "scientific" side, here too a disservice is done to science itself when in its name someone claims for a fact what science cannot prove. This happens when a theory becomes more than a theory or claims to prove more than it can. To say that something is a scientific theory is to place it in its proper context. A theory is not just a guess. Nor is it an actual and final explanation of reality. It is the best explanation that science is capable of providing at a particular time. It is a working hypothesis that proves useful for the time being but, by definition, will be surpassed by other theories that will probably build on it but provide a better explanation of reality. Therefore, to say that evolution is a theory does not mean that it should not be taught as the best possible explanation that we now have as to the origin of species. But it does mean that it should not be taken as the final explanation. Scientists themselves—and not naive believers taking potshots at it—will eventually correct it and surpass it. In fact, in the relatively few years since the publication of Charles Darwin's *The Origin of Species* in 1859, Darwin's theory has been repeatedly refined and corrected. This is good. This is the nature of scientific inquiry. It is on the basis of such theories and their constant refinement and correction that we gain a better understanding of the world and develop technologies that enrich and prolong life—and sometimes also impoverish and destroy it.

Science, however, must deal with facts. When it goes beyond facts it betrays its own nature and it itself loses credibility. This happens, for instance, when scientists claim that the beginning of life happened by chance. There is no way this can ever be observed, proven, or disproved. It does not even provide a particularly useful working hypothesis. All that science can say, if it is true to its own parameters, is that its theories are the best possible explanation of what happened, but whether life is the result of chance or of design, science has no way of telling.

In brief, no service is done to science by extending its good and valid theories into an unscientific claim about matters that are not observable by strict scientific methods. When it comes to the origin of the world and of humankind, science may be very good at suggesting the *how* but has no scientific way to explain, affirm, or deny the *who* or the *for what*.

The *What*: Heaven and Earth

As we look at the two stories in Genesis, the very first thing we find in common between the two is the inclusion of heaven and earth. Genesis 1:1 says that "God began to create the heavens and the earth." The story in Genesis 2 opens with a similar reference to "the day [when] the LORD God made earth and sky" (Gen 2:4b). And between the two, in what may be the end of the first story or the beginning of the second (but in any case provides the connection between the two), we are told that "this is the account of the heavens and the earth when they were created" (Gen 2:4a).

Genesis insists on this point because the various creation stories that circulated at the time spoke of the creation of the world as resulting from conflicts among the gods. This was true of the Babylonian myths that stood at the background of much of what we read in Genesis. It was also true of Greek and Roman mythologies. The gods did not create their abode, the heavens. What they did create, partly as the result of conflicts among themselves, was the earth.

Over against that, Jews as well as Christians insisted that even the heavens are the creation of God. Our God is not part of what exists in heaven, like the gods of Babylonian, Greek, and Roman myths. Our God stands far above both heaven and earth, for both are God's creation.

This view of both heaven and earth as created by God is so central to the Christian faith that the two most widely used creeds among Christians of all confessions open with a reference to it. The very beginning of the Apostles' Creed, probably the best known to most of us, says that "I believe in God the Father Almighty, Maker of heaven and earth." And the Nicene Creed, used not only in Protestant and Catholic Churches but also among the Eastern Churches—Russian, Greek, Ethiopian, Armenian, and several others—declares at its very outset, "We believe in one God the Father Almighty, Maker of heaven and of earth, and of all things visible and invisible."

God is Lord of heaven *and* earth— everything.

We know, however, that the earliest form of the Apostles' Creed, used in the city of Rome early in the second century, did not include the words "Maker of heaven and earth." Why were they added? A simple answer is that practically all the creeds that were developing at the time included this phrase. But this still leaves us with the question: Why did these creeds include such a phrase? The answer is that as Christianity spread beyond the confines of Judaism it encountered stories of creation that did not adjudicate the existence of all things to a single God. Several of these stories spoke of conflicts among the gods and these conflicts resulting in the creation of the world. In consequence, some things in the world were to be ascribed to one god or principle, and others to another. Most commonly, people thought that spiritual reality was good and material reality evil. The physical world was believed to have been created by lesser gods who were either evil or ignorant. It was only the spiritual world that was to be ascribed to a good creator. From this perspective, the human predicament was that we are good spirits trapped in evil bodies.

Jews and Christians would not accept such views. On the contrary, they would insist that there is only one God and that this God is the good and sole Creator of all things. When scripture and the creeds spoke of "heaven and earth," they were not simply listing two things among others. There were rather saying "everything, absolutely everything."

Actually, in a way even before adding that phrase the earliest forms of the Apostles' Creed already implied this view. Notice the *all* in "*All*-mighty." The Greek word that we now translate as "almighty" is *pantokrator*, which literally means "all ruling." The emphasis here is not on a God who can do anything God wishes—which may well be true, but is not the point here—but rather on a God who rules over *everything*. This obviously included the Roman Empire and its rulers and therefore had politically subversive overtones—which it still has! But it also included the physical world of matter and body and thus denied the easy and generally held distinction between a good spiritual reality and an evil, material one.

In affirming their belief in "God the Father Almighty, Maker of heaven and earth," early Christians were declaring that all that exists, material and spiritual, heavenly and earthly, is the result of God's loving act of creation. The God who is love has made heaven and earth out of love. Nothing—absolutely nothing—that exists is not the result of God's love.

This is one of the main reasons why eventually Christians began speaking of creation out of nothing—*creatio ex nihilo*. There is little about this in early Christian theology. But when some began adopting the Greek philosophical teaching of an eternal matter out of which the world is made, Christians in general rejected such views. A preexistent eternal matter would imply that God is not the creator of all, that God is not the sole principle of all.

Back to the *Who*: God Is Love

"God is love," says 1 John 4:8. What does this mean? How far may we carry it? Certainly, part of what John is saying is that God's love is manifested in our redemption through Jesus Christ, and therefore we are to love one another. Thus, "The person who doesn't love doesn't know God, because God is love" (1 John 4:8). God's love is manifested in redemption; and before that in sustenance and provision; and before that, as we have seen, in creation itself. And before that?

Christian doctrine holds that there is only one God. But it also holds that this God exists as three "persons" traditionally called *Father, Son,* and *Holy Spirit*. This is the doctrine of the Trinity. There has been much speculation as to how this is to be understood, what is meant by *person*, and so on. But such speculation has often eclipsed the main point we should draw from the doctrine of the Trinity. This is that even God does not exist in solitary splendor. True love, that which exists in God, is such that even within the one God there is sharing, there is communion; and it is this sharing, this communion, that makes God one.

The essence of God is sharing, communion.

Early last century, as humankind was coming to grips with the ravages of World War I, which manifested the consequences to which a lack of love could lead, Lionel Thornton wrote that

> the law of *agape* [love] reigns in heaven, and only so can be translated to earth.... This law of *agape*...must be referred back to its transcendent source in the life of God.... The fellowship, or *koinonia*, of the Spirit in the new community is referred back to a transcendent fellowship of Persons in the life of God.[2]

And later in the same century, as inequality in Latin America often resulted in violence, Franciscan theologian Leonardo Boff underscored the importance of the doctrine of the Trinity as follows:

> God is Father, Son, and Holy Spirit in reciprocal communion. They coexist from all eternity; none is before or after, or superior or inferior, to the other. Each Person enwraps the others; all permeate one another and live in one another. This is the reality of trinitarian communion, so infinite and deep that the divine Three are united and are therefore one sole God. The divine unity is communitarian because each Person is in communion with the other two.[3]

Thus, even leaving aside all speculation and explanations about the distinctions among the divine persons, one can at least say that the doctrine of the Trinity means that "God is love" not only because God loves us but also and above all because there is love even within the Godhead itself. It is this God who is love whom we call "Father Almighty, Maker of heaven and earth."

A Word on the *How*

While there has been much discussion on the how of creation, this discussion has focused mostly on the seven days over against millions of years, and similar matters. Carried away by such debates, we often miss an important point in the Genesis stories, and that is the power of God's word. This is particularly noticeable in the first creation story in Genesis chapter one, where we are repeatedly told that "God said . . . and there was": "let there be light" (v. 3); "let there be a dome in the middle of the waters" (v. 6); "let the waters under the sky come together" (v. 9); "let the earth grow plant life" (v. 11); "let there be lights in the dome of the sky" (v. 14); "let the waters swarm with of living things" (v. 20); "let the earth produce every kind of living thing" (v. 24). (In the second story, as we shall see in our next chapter, this emphasis on the power of God's word is reflected in the power of human words.)

Not only in Genesis but also throughout scripture, the word of God, God's speech, is much more than mere communication. When God speaks, what God utters springs into existence: "Let there be . . . and there was." This may be seen, for instance, in Isaiah 55:11, where God declares that, just as the rain comes down from heaven and does not return there until it has watered the soil, "so is my word that comes from my mouth; / it does not return to me empty. / Instead, it does what I want, / and accomplishes what I intend." This does not only mean, as we commonly understand, that preaching will be successful. It means that also what God speaks God does, and therefore the promises that God has spoken are absolutely trustworthy.

In a well-known passage, the New Testament reiterates this emphasis on the power of God's word as the means of creation: "In the beginning was the Word / and the Word was with God / and the Word was God. The Word was with God in the beginning. / Everything came into being through the Word, / and without the Word / nothing came into being" (John 1:1-3).

As we shall see in chapter 3, this is important because it will help us understand much of what the creation stories and the rest of the Bible say about human beings and our place in creation.

The Creator's Stamp on Creation

When Armand designs a dress, he leaves his mark on it in two ways: First, at a rather superficial level, necessary only for those who do not know Armand and his work, he puts a label on the dress with his name on it. Second, at a much deeper level, those who know Armand and have seen enough of his work to recognize his creative touch do not really need a label. The dress is Armand's creation simply because it reflects Armand himself. While the explicit words on the label provide for easy recognition, the label itself has value because of who Armand is and what he has done.

Likewise, we may say that we know in two different ways that God is Creator: First, we could say that we know it because God tells us it is so. Clearly, the Bible tells us it is so, and church doctrine confirms it. This sort of assurance is not to be discounted. It is just as important for us as is the Armand label for a prospective buyer. It is the basic assurance that tells us that we may and should look for God's imprint on creation. But then, the more we come to know God the more we see the Creator's stamp on creation. When the psalmist declares that "The heavens are telling the glory of God; / and the firmament proclaims his handiwork" (Ps 19:1 NRSV), this does not mean only that the psalmist believes what he has been told, that God made the heavens and the earth. It means also that the psalmist, having experienced the wisdom and the love of God, now sees that love and that wisdom reflected in the heavens. As any Hebrew, he has been told that the firmament bears the label of God; but as someone who knows God he now sees for himself the hand of God in the heavens. As many biblical scholars tell us, even though both the Bible and the Creeds begin with creation, Israel came to know God first as powerful redeemer and loving liberator, and then, knowing something about this God and God's power, wisdom, and love, they came to see God's hand in all of creation.

Creation shows us God's power, wisdom, and love.

Along these lines, St. Augustine argued—and most medieval theology agreed—that when believers look at creation they see not only signs of God's power and wisdom but also signs of the Trinity—what he called *vestigia trinitatis in creatura*, vestiges of the Trinity in the creature. In his extensive treatise *On the Trinity*, he gave, among other examples, one that later became fairly common: one can see the stamp of the Trinity on the human mind, in which there is intellect, love (or will), and knowledge. From that point, medieval theology took off, seeking vestiges of the Trinity everywhere. They claimed, for instance, that the Trinity was reflected in everything, for all that exists is one, true, and good. And then they proceeded to classify such vestiges, creating an entire hierarchy of them, beginning with the vestige of the Trinity in the sanctified, and moving on down to the vestige of the Trinity even in shadows.

Without going that far, we may say that we see signs of a God who is love in ourselves and in all of creation. We see those signs in the beauty of nature—notwithstanding the presence of violence and evil, to which we shall return. We see them in the sunrise and the sunset, in the mountains and in the ocean, in the stars and in the atoms. But if it is true that the Creator God is love, that love exists within the Godhead itself, then we can also say that we see the imprint of God in the interdependence of all creatures. No creature is able to stand by itself. They all exist in interrelationship. Planets revolve around stars, and electrons around nuclei. While centrifugal forces prevent the collapse of the whole into a single undifferentiated mass, gravity holds it all together—much as love requires at once the gravity of commonality and the centrifugal force of self-identity. Being created in love and for love is particularly true of the human creature, of which according to Genesis 2:18 God said, "It is not good that the man should be alone" (NRSV).

In brief, the doctrine of creation is neither only nor even primarily about origins but rather about relationships: about the relationship between God and the world, between God and us, among us and others, and among all creatures. And all of this bearing the sign of the God who is love.

An Addendum and a Look Forward: Creative Loafing

"On the seventh day God rested," says Genesis 2:2. The Creator loafing! What are we to make of this?

First of all, much to my surprise and against what I have repeatedly thought and said, God's rest on the seventh day implies the autonomy of creation. I have repeatedly said and written that God's act of creation continues to this day; for without God's sustaining power all things would immediately dissolve into nothingness. The first part of that sentence is correct: God's creative action continues to this day. But the second is questionable. Scripture speaks of a God who rests from the work of creation—and the world goes on! This is a God so powerful as to be able to create a world that remains in existence even while God rests!

Second, and as a consequence of the first point, God's rest is an expression of God's love. As was said at the beginning of this essay, God is willing to create another reality—other realities—vis-à-vis Godself. Thanks to creation, other beings exist—beings that are other than God. And God's love is such as to allow these beings to subsist on their own—to subsist even while God rests. In other words, while God creates and therefore possesses the whole of creation, God's love is not possessive or dominant.

Third, this means that the "otherness" of God goes both ways. As a reaction to liberalism, which tended to speak of God as some sort of superhuman and to confuse human capabilities with divine power, theologians in the twentieth century took to speaking of God as "the wholly other." This was an important corrective, which must not be forgotten. But God's rest, and the autonomy of creation, means that we too are "wholly others" vis-à-vis God. The distance between Creator and creator must be stressed not only to make it clear that God is sovereign, holy, unapproachable except by divine revelation. It must also be stressed to make it clear that in creating us God has decided that there will be other beings besides Godself, that God has given us autonomy, that God gives us space to be ourselves.

Fourth, God's rest means that we must not take our work too seriously. The God who is able to let go and rest invites and expects us also to let go and rest. If creation is able to keep going while God rests, it will certainly keep going while we rest! As we continue in our study, we shall see that we have been given much authority and much responsibility in this creation of God's. We must take this seriously. But we must also acknowledge that we need rest and that creation does not really need for us to be constantly active. (Although I must confess that this is not always a word that I heed. Right now, it is a Sunday afternoon, most of my friends are watching football, and I am sitting at my computer, typing away!)

Finally, there is a **fifth** point that follows from God's rest: God is not always available to us, at our beck and call. As we shall see further on, to say that ours is a God who rests implies also that ours is a God who is not always available. In the Genesis story, God is not right there to tell the man and the woman not to fall to the wiles of the serpent. God plants the garden, creates the human couple, gives them directions, and then seems to leave them to their own devices. To this we shall return, for it is the very foundation of Christian stewardship.

Discussion Questions

1. Reread the first three chapters of Genesis. What jumps out at you today? Briefly compare the two creation stories. Which story do you prefer? Why might there be two different stories of creation in the Bible?

2. What does it mean that the greatest act of God's love is taking a risk on us? Share a time when you took a risk. Are you typically a risk-tolerant or risk-adverse person?

3. The author says that what should concern us about creation is not *how* the world was made but *who* made it. Is this true for you? Why do people argue over the *how*?

4. The author says that the "doctrine of creation is neither only nor even primarily about origins but rather about relationships: about the relationship between God and the world, between God and us, among us and others, and among all creatures." Share a time when you felt close to God. How do you see God reflected in nature? In other people? In yourself?

The Human Creature

Let Us Make Humans in Our Image, according to Our Likeness

One point on which the two stories in Genesis agree is that humankind is the culmination of creation. In the first story, humankind is created on the sixth day, after which God rests. In the second, the man is created first, then the plants and the animals—which are created in order to provide company to the man, but are not able to achieve that goal—and finally the story culminates in the creation of the woman.

But before we deal with the place of humans in creation, a word must be said about the plural *us* that God uses in Genesis 1:26, "Let *us* make humanity in *our* image to resemble *us*" (emphasis added). This use of the plural has been interpreted in various ways. To some it is simply a sign that the story has been drawn from polytheistic creation stories and that here God is in dialogue with other celestial beings. This is hardly believable for it is clear that the biblical writer has taken great care to delete all polytheistic references in the narratives he (or she) has borrowed and adapted from other sources, and it would be most improbable to retain a single such reference almost at the very beginning of the story. Other interpreters suggest that this plural is intended to stress the majesty of God, much as kings use the "royal we"—as in "it has come to our attention" or "we command." If this is the case, by using this plural the text intends to show that what is about to be made is of particular interest to the supreme ruler of all. Then, in much of Christian tradition, the plural "let us" has been interpreted as a sign of the Trinity consulting within itself. In the fourth century, Gregory of Nyssa saw the *us* as a sign of the importance of this new being, whose creation required thought and consultation ("let us make") in contrast to all other creatures ("let there be"). We shall hear echoes of this interpretation in some of the references that are to follow. A view not often mentioned, but found in ancient Jewish commentaries, is that in the *us* God is inviting the earth to be part of this act of creation. Having made the earth, the heavens, and all that is within them, God affirms their significance by bringing that whole creation into a conversation about the creation of humans. And this in itself is a sign of the importance of these human beings who are about to be made in a unique collaboration between God and creation itself. Whatever the case may be, it is clear that there is something special about this creature that God proposes to place on earth.

Along these lines, the above-mentioned Gregory of Nyssa declares that the reason why in this biblical narrative humans are created last is that all the rest of creation was the work of God preparing a place for them. He says that "it was not to be looked for that the ruler should appear before the subjects of his rule," and that therefore in the rest of creation God was acting as a good host preparing a place for the human guests:

[For] as a good host does not bring his guest to his house before the preparation of his feast, but, when he has made all due preparation, and decked with their proper adornments his house...in the same manner the rich and munificent Entertainer of our nature, when He had decked the habitation with beauties of every kind, and prepared this great and varied banquet, then introduced man.[1]

There has been much more discussion also on the subject of the image of God. Nineteenth-century scholars of a liberal bent claimed that this was no more than an expression of anthropomorphism, of thinking that God looks much like us, and that it is therefore simply a sign of the primitive nature of Hebrew religion. Such scholars argued that all of Israel's neighbors had gods shaped after people and animals, and therefore Israel's God, while being only one, was conceived in a way similar to those neighboring gods.

Along different lines of thought, from ancient times to the present some have tried to discover the difference between the "image" and the "likeness," saying for instance that the first is to be seen in human reason and the second in the ability to relate to God. To this scholars have properly responded that what we have here is an instance of the sort of poetic parallelism that is typical of Hebrew and other ancient literature where a single idea is repeated in different words. (Look for instance at Psalm 1, where you will note that in almost every verse the same idea is expressed in two parallel phrases or images.)

Many early Christian writers joined the verse in Genesis 1:26 with Colossians 1:15, where Paul affirms that Christ "is the image of the invisible God" and came to the conclusion that Jesus Christ was the model that God used for the creation of humankind. In other words, God always intended to be fully joined with the human creature and therefore used that intended union—God's incarnation in Jesus—as the model after which humanity was created. This may be seen, for instance, in the writings of Irenaeus of Lyon, a second-century theologian long underestimated but currently gaining influence, who affirmed that the Word of God "was manifested when the Word of God was made man, assimilating Himself to man. . . . For in times long past, it was said that man was created after the image of God, but it was not actually shown; for the Word was as yet invisible, after whose image man was created."[2]

Similar views persisted throughout the Middle Ages, when theologians debated whether, had there been no sin, God would have become incarnate. Although the general consensus was that the main purpose of the incarnation was to undo the result of sin—a view that eventually became prevalent—this was by no means clear to all. There certainly was full agreement that the incarnation was a remedy for sin. But was this all it was? Or was it rather part of God's eternal plan—the plan of a God whose love for humankind is such as to wish to be united with us and become one of us? St. Thomas Aquinas, without any doubt the most influential theologian after St. Augustine, tackled the question and came to the conclusion that, while he believed that the incarnation was solely a remedy for sin, the opposite view was also tenable. He says,

> On this matter there are different opinions. Some say that the Son of God would have become incarnate even if humans had not sinned. Others hold to the opposite. The latter opinion seems most reasonable. . . . The incarnation was ordained by God as a remedy to sin, and therefore, were

there no sin to redeem, there would be no incarnation. Yet the power of God is such that it is not limited by this, and therefore God could have become incarnate even had there been no sin.[3]

In more recent times, Jesuit theologian and paleontologist Pierre Teilhard de Chardin spoke of Christ as the "omega point" toward which all creation is evolving. According to Teilhard, all evolution is "an ascent towards consciousness,"[4] and its culmination is the joining of all things at the omega point toward which evolution moves, God incarnate in Jesus Christ.

Jesus is not only God's response to sin but the culmination of creation.

This may seem strange to us for we have generally been taught that according to the Bible God made the human creature perfect, that then sin and the fall intervened, and that as a response to sin God decided to take flesh. But this was not the only view in the early church, nor is it the only way in which the biblical record may be read and construed. For Irenaeus, and for many other Christians then and through the ages, God always intended for creation to develop, for humans to till the earth and build cities, and eventually to become very closely united with God. In this Christian tradition, quite ancient and often forgotten, the incarnation of God in Jesus is not only a response to sin, but also the culmination of creation, the point for which all creation was made and toward which creation is moving.

Dominion

Even leaving aside such inspiring possibilities, it is clear that in Genesis 1:26 the notion of the image and likeness of God is closely related to dominion. What God says is, "Let us make humankind in our image, according to our likeness, and let them have dominion." And then God goes on to list what has previously been created: fish, birds, domestic and wild animals, placing it all under human dominion. In the second story, something similar is said. There God makes first the man and then brings the animals to the man so that he may name them. The act of naming is a claim of authority over the named. (Interestingly, today we speak of people's names as their "handles," which seems to imply that in some ways a name is still a form of control.) Therefore, according to the two stories in Genesis as well as elsewhere in the Bible (see for instance Ps 8) the human creature is given dominion over the rest of creation.

To be made after the image of God is also to be God's representatives. In ancient times, it was common to value the image of a king not only as a reminder of the ruler but also as his representative so that it was due a respect similar to that owed to the king himself. We have an interesting example of this in Daniel 3, where Nebuchadnezzar commands that a huge statue of himself made out of gold is to be adored by all. Likewise, at the time of the birth of Christianity, people all over the Roman Empire were expected to burn incense before the ruler's image as a sign of loyalty. To disrespect the image of the ruler was to disrespect the ruler himself and was considered an act of sedition. In the late Middle Ages we hear echoes of this in the legend of William Tell where the foreign ruler had his hat raised on a pole and ordered that all must bow before it. To show lack of respect for the hat was to show lack of respect for the ruler. And today, when a flag represents a nation, to insult the flag is to insult the nation.

To be made in God's image is to be God's representative, to have God-like dominion over creation. And it means also that to desecrate this image is no less than an attack on God! This has been a common point in Christian preaching and teaching and in Christian calls for love and justice. For instance, in the fourth century, Gregory of Nyssa attacked the practice of slavery as a desecration of the image of God: "You say, 'I have bought male and female slaves.' Tell me, ... how many coins do you think the image of God is worth? For how much money did you carry away this nature created by God?"[5]

Returning to the matter of human dominion over creation we need to confess that this notion has led to much abuse. Native American Vine Deloria is not entirely wrong when he blames much of the despoliation of the earth on this Judeo-Christian claim that humankind is to have dominion over creation. He says,

> Whether or not Christians wanted to carry their doctrine of man's dominance as far as it has been carried, the fact remains that the modern world is just beginning to identify the Christian religion's failure to show adequate concern for the planet as a major factor in our present ecological crisis.[6]

Humans are to treat the creation with the same love that God has for us.

But this is not the entire picture. In fact, what Genesis says is that the dominion that the human creature is to have over the rest of creation is dominion after the image and likeness of God's dominion. Lutheran professor Terence E. Fretheim explains that neither the "dominion" envisioned here, nor the commandment to "subdue" the earth in verse 28, are to be understood as a license to exploit the earth:

> A study of the verb *have dominion* reveals that it must be understood in terms of care-giving, even nurturing, not exploitation. As the image of God, human beings should relate to the nonhuman as God relates to them.... More generally, "subduing" involves development in the created order. This process offers to the human being the task of... bringing the world along to its fullest possible creational potential.[7]

Just as God creates the world out of love, so must the human creature, as the representative of God's dominion, manage the world in love. And just as in the creative act God created another reality and gave it the power and the freedom to be itself, so humans, as God's representatives and reflecting God's dominion, must respect the otherness of the rest of creation. As we shall see in another chapter, this is what is commonly known as "stewardship."

To have dominion over the earth means that we manage the world with love, not exploit it with greed.

It is important to note, however, that this management involves a process, a development, as Fretheim says. The notion that God created humankind and placed it in Eden to do nothing, popular as it is, is quite the opposite of what Genesis says. Contrariwise to what is often said, in the book of Genesis labor is not a curse or a punishment for sin. In the first creation story, no matter how perfect, the earth still had to be tilled and subdued (Gen 1:28). And exactly the same point is made in the second story, where "God took the man and put him in the Garden of Eden to till it and keep it" (Gen 2:15 NRSV). Even though our commonly held view is that Genesis speaks of a creation that is already finished and was intended to remain always as it was, the biblical text itself says otherwise. The earth is to be tilled. The garden is to be tended. As we shall see in another chapter, it is significant that the story that begins in Genesis in a garden ends in a city in Revelation.

Out of the Earth

In the second creation story, the relationship of the human creature to the earth is twofold. On the one hand, the man is to till the garden and keep it—that is, to be its manager. But on the other, he is made out of the ground. "Then the LORD God formed man from the dust of the ground, and breathed into his nostrils the breath of life; and the man became a living being" (Gen 2:7 NRSV). But it is not only the man who is made from the dust of the ground. "So the LORD God formed from the fertile land all the wild animals and all the birds in the sky" (Gen 2:19). No matter what dominion or responsibility this human creature is to have over the rest of creation, it is still part of creation. Whatever we say about creation must include ourselves. We are made of the same earth as are the cattle, the birds, and the wolves—which means that St. Francis was right when he spoke of "brother wolf"! This may be seen in the very proximity between the name given to the human, *adam*, and the name of the dirt from which he is made, *adamah*. (In English, we have a similar connection between *human* and *humus*.)

Reinhold Niebuhr expressed this in terms of a paradox that stands at the very center of what it means to be human. He tells us that there are two facts about human beings that must be affirmed at the same time:

> The obvious fact is that man is a child of nature, subject to its vicissitudes, propelled by its necessities, driven by its impulses, and confined within the brevity of the years nature permits....The other less obvious fact is that man is a spirit who stands outside of nature, life, himself, his reason, and the world.[8]

Niebuhr then goes on to point out "how difficult it is to do justice to both the uniqueness of man and his affinities with the world of nature."[9]

It is this dual identity in humankind that both distinguishes us from the rest of creation and makes us part of it. We are part of the animal kingdom. Our physical needs and bodily functions are very similar to those of a cow, a pig, or an eagle. We can be classified as part of the animal kingdom: within that kingdom, as vertebrates; among vertebrates, as mammals; among mammals, as hominids. Now it is even possible to transplant parts of animal bodies into our own. There is no doubt that we are made of the same dirt as the elephant and the cockroach.

But that is not all we are. Among all these animals, we seem to be the only ones that have a sense of transcendence. We can stand outside ourselves and look at ourselves. We can question who we are. We can plan what we hope to become. We can rejoice in what we have done, and we can weep over it. We can set goals. We can dream of things and conditions that do not exist and then bring them to reality. We can look at our fellow creatures and plan to make something new and better out of them—or deface and destroy them.

We may even say that we are the only creature that seems to have the freedom to become what it is not. Humans can become inhuman, but a cat, an ox, or a dog cannot become "unfeline," "unbovine," or "uncanine." This is our blessing, and also our potential curse.

There is a story about two astronomers talking. One says to the other, "From the point of view of astronomy, we are but worms." To which the other responds, "From the point of view of astronomy, we are the astronomers." Paradoxically, they are both right. We may try to deny one of these two dimensions of our existence. Thus, some say that "life is short," and take this as an excuse to live purely carnal lives, enjoying the moment, eating, drinking, and being merry. Others may take the opposite direction, saying that, precisely because life is short, it must be lived as the spiritual beings we are, preparing for eternity, and paying little or no attention to the animal or physical side of our nature. But neither will succeed. Those who seek to live as if they were mere dirt will still dream, evaluate, plan. And those who seek to live as if they were purely spiritual beings will still need to eat. Using the terminology of Genesis, we are dirt shaped after the image of God.

It Is Not Good That the Man Should Be Alone

In the first creation story, after each step of creation, God looks upon each thing that has been made and sees that it is good (Gen 1:4, 10, 12, 18, 21, 25). Then, once everything is made—including the first humans—we are told that "God saw everything that he had made: it was supremely good" (Gen 1:31). But in the second story, where God makes the man first, God then says, "It is *not good* that the man should be alone; I will make him a helper as his partner" (Gen 2:18 NRSV, emphasis added). The eventual result is the creation of the woman out of the man's rib.

> Man and woman: partners, helpers, coworkers—the same substance, the same purpose—different aspects of the same image.

Since "it is not good that the man should be alone," God decides to make him "a helper as his partner" (Gen 2:18 NRSV). Unfortunately, the two words, *helper* and *partner*, have frequently been seriously misinterpreted. The word translated as *helper* is most commonly used in the Bible in the sense of a strong help. Indeed, it is frequently applied to God, as in "God is our helper." The word translated as *partner* literally means "as in front of him"—apparently as a mirror image. It means "fitting" or "appropriate." The King James Version translated this second word as *meet*, which at time meant fitting—as in the old liturgical response to the call to give thanks to God: "It is meet and right so to do." This was a correct translation. But from the King James Version's two words, *help meet*, the word *helpmeet* evolved, which has very different connotations, tending to imply weakness and inferiority—which is exactly the opposite of what the text actually says.

It is at this point that naming comes into the picture. God makes all the animals (birds, cattle, and the wild beasts), apparently as potential helpers fitting to the man, and brings them before the man so that he can name them—that is, so that he can claim power and authority over them. This the man does, but in the end "there was not found a helper as his partner" (Gen 2:20 NRSV).

This leads to the well-known episode of the rib. The intent of this story is to make it clear that the relationship between the man and the woman is different than the relationship between the man and all other living things. Although quite often having been made out of the man's rib has been interpreted as a sign of dependence or subordination, the opposite is the truth. All other living creatures—including the man himself—are made directly out the dust of the earth. Not so the woman, who is made from the very substance of the man—although this too is dirt. Upon being presented to her, the man declares that "this one finally is bone from my bones / and flesh from my flesh" (Gen 2:23) and then refuses to give her a separate name—which would have been a claim of authority over her. Instead, he shares his name with her: he is *ish*, and she will be *ishsah*. It is only later, after sin has intervened, that he calls her "Eve," thus claiming power and authority over her (Gen 3:20).

If having read this second story we return to the matter of the image of God in humans, another dimension may be added: part of what it means to be human is that it is not good for us to be alone. We have been created for community by the God who *is* community. We have been created to love by the God who *is* love, the triune God. The image of God in us includes both the capacity and the need to love and to be loved. Alone, we are not what we are supposed to be. From the moment of our birth we are dependent on others; for alone we cannot even feed ourselves. Being in community with others is so central to our being that solitary confinement is considered cruel and unusual punishment and may eventually lead to madness. Even among Christians, throughout the history of the church there have been many saintly people who sought to live a holy life in solitude and came to the conclusion that true holiness is grounded in love and that love cannot exist in absolute isolation from others. As John Wesley said, the very phrase, "a solitary saint," is contradictory, for it is impossible to be a saint by oneself.

Creative Creatures

As we read these stories, it is clear that the human creature is depicted as being itself creative. Not only do humans have dominion over the earth; they also have the responsibility to till and thus improve it. According to the Genesis stories, humans were placed on earth to represent God's dominion—a dominion of love.

This is why humans have the power of speech, which we may use as a way to claim dominion—as does the man in naming the animals. This too reflects the image of the God who made all things by means of speech—or by means of the word.

Very early Christian writers speculated that in God there is an "unuttered" and an "uttered" speech. In an unuttered form, God knows all possibilities; but it is only that which God utters that comes into existence. Just as God's creation takes place when God's thought is uttered as speech, humans act by uttering their thoughts. Humans, like God, have the power to create new realities and to shape old ones. And this power is often applied by means of speech. As long as our words are unuttered, they remain within us, and we still have the freedom to utter them or not. But once they are uttered their power is unleashed—a power such that they can never be taken back and leashed as if they had never been spoken.

In our modern society we tend to underestimate the power of speech. We teach our children to say, "Sticks and stones may hurt my bones, but words will never harm me." But the fact is that words can be more painful than sticks and stones. Many of us, as we look back at our childhood days, will remember scrapes and fights in which we were hurt. But we also remember hurtful words that were said to us—by another child, by a teacher, by a parent—and their hurt still remains. Words are powerful. Tell a child, over and over again, that she is mean and irresponsible, and you will probably create a woman who is indeed mean and irresponsible. Tell another that he is sweet, loving, and responsible, and you will create a man who is indeed sweet, loving, and responsible.

Human words, like God's word, but to a much lesser degree, are powerful. Humans can use the power of their words to create—to create community, to organize society, to develop ideas, to bring them to fruition. Or, as is often the case, we can use that power to destroy, to falsify, to divide. Something beautiful is created when we say, "I love you." And something ugly is created when we say, "I loathe you." In both we are using the power given to us after the likeness of the Creator God. But in one we are using this power as God intends, and in the other we are not—which leads us directly into the thorny questions of sin and the existence of evil.

Discussion Questions

1. We often talk about people worrying about the kind of image they portray. How important is image and status in your church? What is the community's image of your church? What kind of reputation does your church have? How important is a person's reputation? What kinds of things damage or bolster a person's image or reputation?

2. How can we be God's representatives in our world? Share a time when someone represented you or when you represented someone (for example, your family, your business, your friend). When someone represents you, what do you expect?

3. Discuss the power of words. What kinds of words are helpful and hurtful? Share a time when someone told you they loved you. Think and talk about ways that God shows us God's love.

Enter Evil

So far it all sounds beautiful. Creation is about multi-colored sunsets, and twinkling stars, and gurgling brooks, and singing birds, and beautiful spring days...

But this is not all there is. This is a world of earthquakes, tsunamis, hurricanes, drought, floods, and volcanoes. A world in which millions die of AIDS or of starvation. A world in which people kill one another for a pair of shoes while others fly planes to smash into buildings and kill thousands in the name of religion. A world in which Muslims kill Christians, and Christians kill Muslims, and Catholics kill Protestants, and Protestants kill Catholics—all in the name of God!

Many of us find evil so unbearable that we hide from it. Since my community is fairly quiet, I hide from the wars and rumors of wars that pervade our world. Since my immediate neighbors and I have plenty to eat, I try not to know that there are children starving both near and far. True evil is so corrosive that I take refuge in the fake evil of TV shows where everything is eventually solved, and there are no hard feelings, and they all live happily ever after—shows in which even murder is entertaining, as a sort of puzzle to solve and not a tragedy to mourn.

But we cannot really hide. Evil is not just over there but also here, right next to me and even inside me.

We affirm God's power, God's love, and the reality of evil.

The Problem of Evil: Theodicy

The problem of evil is usually referred to as *theodicy*, a word derived from *theos*, "God," and *dikaios*, "just." Thus, it can be briefly stated as the problem of how there can be evil in a world created by a just God. Imagine a triangle whose apex, angle A, is "God's power." At the base, angle B is "God's love," and angle C is "The reality of evil." For Christians, the problem is that we affirm all three, and yet we cannot reconcile them. How can an almighty, loving God, create a world in which there is evil?

The problem is easily solved by eliminating angles A and B. There is no God—neither an almighty nor a loving one. We are simply left to our own devices in a world where evil and violence reign. While this sounds harsh, it is under such premises that most of our society works. In a world of economic, political, social, and even religious competition, many say, "Let me take what I can, and the Devil—if there is such a thing—take the hindmost." Or, as is often stated, "Do unto others before they do unto you." Evil reigns and will forever reign.

One may reach similar consequences by simply eliminating angle B. In this view, God is powerful, but does not love. Some have said, for instance, that the world is like a machine that God set in motion, but now it simply runs on its own, and God does not care what happens to it or in it. If the world is understood as such a machine, even though one may try to distance God from actual events, ultimately, since God is the one who built the machine, God is responsible for whatever happens in it. No matter how powerful, the God who created the world is not a loving God and does not oppose evil. Again, evil reigns.

Then, one may try to solve the problem by eliminating angle A. In that case, God loves but is not powerful. In relatively recent times, some theologians, making use of the theology of process, have sought to explain evil by declaring that, since all is in process, God is in process and has not yet come to the fullness of power. Evil shows that God is not almighty. At various points in history, there have been those who have followed a similar path. One way to do this is to say that God did not create out of nothing but rather out of a preexistent matter. In that case the cause of evil is the recalcitrant matter with which God has to deal. Or, as the Manichees did almost two millennia ago, some have claimed that the true picture includes only angles B and C and that these two are eternal principles of equal power: good and evil, or spirit and matter, or light and darkness. Since these two principles are eternal, the most that can be hoped for is a final separation between the two so that good will no longer be mingled with evil as it is at present.

Much more common, particularly among modern believers, is to weaken angle C—the reality of evil—to such a point that there is no evil but only a semblance of it. Thus, when something evil happens, we say, "We do not really understand. What appears evil to us is in fact good. God knows why this happens, and this too is part of God's plan." In other words, what seems evil to us is not really such. It is part of God's good actions. Like a shot at the doctor's office, it might be unpleasant, but it is actually for our own good. And, like a young child having a shot, we may cry, protest, and wonder if our parent really loves us. But eventually we shall understand that it was all for our own good.

This may satisfy us when we look at relatively minor events that thwart what we thought was good. It may also explain why there are flies and mosquitoes—perhaps they have a useful purpose after all. But is it hardly satisfying to a mother who grieves because her child was killed by a drunk driver or to any who take thought of the thousands of children starving every day all over the world.

J. L. Mackie has stated these options rather succinctly:

> If you are prepared to say that God is not wholly good, or not quite omnipotent, or that evil does not exist, or that good is not opposed to the kind of evil that exists, or that there are limits to what an omnipotent being can do, then the problem of evil does not arise for you.[1]

Christians, however, are not willing to let go of any of these points. Each corner of the triangle described above is crucial to our faith. We affirm that God is powerful, that God is loving, and that evil is real. Therefore, we must openly and unashamedly confess that we do not understand evil. But then we must also recognize that this is precisely what makes evil be such. Evil is senseless, purposeless. Paul refers to it as "the *mystery* of lawlessness" (2 Thess 2:7 NRSV, emphasis added). Ultimately, we cannot explain evil. We cannot understand it. If we could, it would simply go away. Evil is not just a puzzle to solve. It is, to use a well-known cliché, a mystery wrapped in an enigma. It is fraught with paradoxes. It is unexplainable and yet inescapable. It is precisely this that makes it be evil.

Facing the Mystery

To say that evil is a mystery is not to say that we are to let it go at that and not struggle with the mystery itself. Because it is a mystery we know that we can never solve it. But because we must constantly struggle with it we must still do all we can to understand its various dimensions.

This was one of the main problems that young Augustine had back in the fourth century. His mother, Monica, was a devout Christian and had sought to raise him in the faith. Augustine himself was torn between his mother's faith and his own difficulties to accept it. He certainly had moral and behavioral difficulties with what he felt Christian faith would demand of him. But he also had intellectual difficulties. Foremost among these was the question of evil. How could Monica's loving and powerful God be the Creator of so many evil things?

This puzzlement led Augustine to Manicheism, which claimed that there is not one eternal principle in the world, but two. One is good, and the other is evil. One is spiritual, and the other is material. One is light, and the other is darkness. The present predicament is that these two principles are intermingled. This is the case not only with the world at large but also with human beings in whom a spiritual spark is trapped in a material body, and therefore there is a constant struggle between light and darkness. In the end, when the two are separated, these spiritual sparks will be freed from their enslavement to matter.

Although Augustine flirted with these ideas for some time and sought enlightenment from the Manichees, in the end he found their views unsatisfactory.

His eventual "solution" was twofold. First, he came to the conclusion that nothing—literally meaning no-thing—is in itself evil. Everything that exists is good, and true, and beautiful, as long as it is in its place. A monkey, for instance, it beautiful as a monkey, a complex and harmonious reality much to be admired. But a human that looks like a monkey is not beautiful. This means that evil is not a substance. It is not a "thing." Rather, it is a misplacement of good things, a corruption of the good, a disorder in the good world that God has created.

But, what is the origin of such disorder? It certainly cannot be God. It is here that Augustine brings in the second element of his response: free will. Among the many good things that God has created, there are some that can never be perverted—the virtues. These he calls the "greater goods." Then, there are many that, while being good, are often put to evil use—the body, money, power, and so on. These are the "lesser goods." Between these two categories, free will is an "intermediate good." It is a good because it has been created by God and can do good in imitation and obedience to God. It is intermediate because it can be used for either good or evil.

According to Augustine, a central characteristic of free will is that it is its own cause. Certainly, outside factors, experiences, needs, perceptions, and so on do influence our decisions. But whatever in a decision is determined by outside influences is not truly ours. Decisions are *ours* only inasmuch as they are

generated by the will itself. Thus, one may well say that part of
the image of God in us is that our will, like God's, is ultimately
self-generated. No matter how much prompted by outside
forces, in the final analysis it is not generated by such forces.
This is precisely the reason why we call it "free."

Free will is an intermediate good because we can use it for
good or for evil. In the latter case, the will uses the lesser goods
in an inappropriate way. Most commonly, what we do is to
take what are in fact lesser goods and raise them to the stature
of the higher goods, or even to the level of the divine, thus creating the disorder that is the essence of evil. Power, for instance,
is good, but when we place it at a wrong level in our scale of
values it becomes evil—much as the beauty of a monkey, if
present in a human, becomes ugly.

An example from the natural world may clarify this point.
Scientists tell us that there are moths that normally use the
light of the moon to guide their flight. As long as the moon
remains at the same angle of vision, the moth is flying in a generally straight line. But then a candle appears. It is far less powerful than the moon, but its proximity makes it brighter. The
moth tries to keep the candle at a constant angle of vision, with
the result that it flies in a spiral constantly bringing it closer
to the candle and eventually to death. The moon is good. The
candle is good. But by taking the candle to be the moon the
moth has flown to its own destruction. Likewise, money and
power are good as long as they remain in their place within the
order of life. But when they are taken for the higher good—as
the wayward moth takes the candle—they lead to destruction.

Thus, in brief, Augustine would say that the cause of evil
is free will, which itself is good, but which can be used for evil

and can make good things evil by placing them at a level where they do not belong—or, as Augustine would say, by abusing or misusing them.

However, helpful as this may be, it only touches what one might call moral evil. This is evil resulting from human decision. But there is also natural evil—evil not resulting from human decision but from the forces of nature. It is true that in some cases human decision contributes to such evil. Such is the case, for instance, when poor people lose their land and are forced to live in areas prone to flooding. When the flood comes, people who were forced to move to the area drown. In this case, perhaps the flood would not have been evil were it not for human action. But the fact remains that there is much evil that cannot be attributed to human decision: earthquakes, tsunamis, droughts, storms, viruses...

> # Human actions have real consequences in the short- and long-term, for us and for others.

Augustine and much traditional theology would explain such evil by declaring that human action has consequences for the creation over which we have been placed. Thus, in Genesis God declares that the land will be cursed as a result of human sin. There is much to be said for that. In our own twenty-first century we are witnessing vast natural destruction that can be laid at the door of our past actions and our wanton exploitation of earth's resources. But this is not to say that all natural evil can really be attributed to human sin. On the contrary, there is every indication that long before any humans trod the earth there were earthquakes, volcanoes, and cataclysmic occurrences in which thousands of species and entire ecosystems were destroyed. Given what we now know of the origins of the universe and of the human species, to say that all evil is the consequence of human sin is hardly believable.

In consequence, helpful as Augustine and his entire theological tradition may be, evil is still a mystery. We may try to understand it. We may try to explain it away. We may lay the blame at the feet of Satan. But even so, we know that it remains a conundrum we cannot solve. And, to make matters worse, it is not only unexplainable but also inescapable.

A Creation in Travail

This is a common experience for all Christians. In Romans 8, Paul speaks of creation being "subjected to frustration" (v. 20), of its "slavery to decay" (v. 21), and of its "suffering labor pains" (v. 22). This is a passage to which we shall return in our last chapter; but for the present it serves as an indication of the depth of the power of evil throughout creation. We know that there is much evil within ourselves—in our thoughts, in our decisions, and in our actions. But we also know that there is also much evil "out there," in a world of fang and claw, of storm and flood. Clearly, if God is good, creation is not what God wishes it to be.

How do we explain this? We do not, and we cannot. But we can find metaphors that, while not doing away with the mystery, allow us to acknowledge it and to voice it.

One of these metaphors—the most common throughout Christian history—is "the fall." This metaphor, drawing mostly from the narratives in the first chapters of Genesis, speaks of a primeval time when all was as it should be. In its simplest form, this metaphor speaks of an idyllic "garden of Eden" in which God placed the first human beings. All was provided for them, with no great toil or difficulty, and they were given freedom to eat of the garden, except for the fruit of a certain forbidden tree. They disobeyed, and the result was that not only they but also the entire creation over which they were given dominion was cursed. This is the reason why now the earth does not always produce what we will, why we must toil in order to eat, and why there are such things as pain in childbirth. And, if this metaphor does not suffice to explain why there is evil even where the hand of humans does not reach, it can easily be expanded by speaking of a cosmic fall even before Adam and Eve when one of the angels sinned and thus became the Evil One, Satan, who is the root of all evil. While this metaphor claims to be no more than a repetition of the narratives in Genesis, it goes beyond those narratives and in some points seems to ignore them. First, in Genesis work is not a curse. On the contrary, as we have seen, in both narratives the human creature is to till the earth and subdue it—which implies that the earth is already rebellious or at least not all it should be. And, second, the connection of the serpent in Eden with Satan or with a fallen angel can only be established by means of a series of leaps connecting the serpent in Eden with other passages that speak of Satan or of fallen angels.

In any case, we now know that there was violence on the earth long before there were humans, and therefore we must acknowledge that the fall can be only a metaphoric way of speaking of the origin of evil.

Still, this metaphor is valuable inasmuch as it clearly reminds us that creation is not as God wills it to be. Nature may be beautiful, but it is also cruel. The big fish eats the small fish both in the sea and in human society and business. As Paul said, the entire creation groans as in travail because in its bondage to decay it is not able to be what it should be.

"No Longer," or "Not Yet"?

There is, however, another metaphor that also appeared early in Christian history. While the metaphor of the fall sees evil in terms of "no longer," this other metaphor sees it in terms of "not yet." Within this metaphor, evil is not to be seen mostly as a fall from a primeval perfection, but rather as the present situation of a creation that is still moving to its completion. This was the view of the aforementioned Pierre Teilhard de Chardin, who saw the union of the divine and the human in the incarnation as the "omega point," the final goal toward which all is moving and that gives us a hint of the goal of the present evolution—one fraught with pain and death, and tooth and claw, but still in a mysterious and unseen way moving toward its goal. There are also hints of this in the passage from Romans cited earlier, where Paul speaks of a creation "groaning in travail," as in the pangs of childbirth. For a woman in travail, her pains are not a matter of "no longer," but rather of "not yet."

This other metaphor was quite common in the early church. Among ancient Christian theologians, such views are most notable in the writings of Irenaeus of Lyons in the second century.

It is interesting to note that when Irenaeus speaks of the creation stories in Genesis he does not say "in creation," but rather "at the *beginning* of creation." Like most Christians at the time, he took these stories rather literally. But he saw them not as the story of a completed creation but rather as the story of the beginning of a process that would eventually lead to Jesus and then to the final reign of God. Thus, he says that Adam and Eve were created "as children," meaning that they were perfect as a newborn is perfect but were still intended to grow as a child is intended to grow. They were placed in the garden in order to "learn justice" being taught by the Word of God—meaning by that the Word of which we read in John 1, through whom all things were made and who is the light that enlightens everyone who comes to this world. Their sin made them slaves to evil, and therefore human history is a process of growth twisted by violence and destruction. But it is still growth that God is leading to the intended end—a road beset by obstacles and detours but still leading to the final day when the close union between the divine and the human will be similar to that which we have seen in the incarnation of God in Jesus and was the model or image after which God made humankind.

We live between the "no longer" and the "not yet."

Surprising as this may seem for those of us who have repeatedly heard of the fall, and thus have received the impression that in the Bible and in Christian doctrine the human predicament must be seen as a "no longer," once one recognizes this other metaphor of the "not yet" one sees it throughout scripture. Note, for instance, that the story that begins in a garden in Genesis leads to a city in Revelation. Both the garden and the city are the work of God: the former at the very beginning of creation, and the latter at the end, when the Holy City descends from heaven. Thus, the process leading from a garden to a city—from simple nature to civilization—is not in itself evil. Humans were always intended to till the land, to grow in their understanding of the world, to use this understanding of the created world to "subdue it" and to organize social life. Evil is manifested in that this process is not straightforward but is convoluted, twisted, full of tragedy and destruction. But it is still growth—and God intends growth. To use a common example, our increased understanding of atomic structure is good, and has led to many improvements in human life, but is has also led to incredibly destructive weapons and to mass deaths.

The Depth of the Problem

When Augustine spoke of free will as the cause of evil, he was pointing to a difficult truth to accept: even our will is not what it is supposed to be. Evil is not only "out there." It is also within us. It is so embedded in us that even our will is twisted. We all know from personal experience that when we wish to do something, and we know we should not, we tend to find ways to rationalize it. We tell ourselves, for instance, "I know this is normally wrong; but this is a special case." Or, "Even though I feel bad about doing this, I will feel better later." Or, "Everybody else does it, so why not me?" And the sad fact is that we do succeed in convincing ourselves that what we do is not really all that bad!

Since our will is not what it should be, our dominion over creation also is not what it should be. This too we rationalize, telling ourselves that, since nature does not do what we wish it would, we ought to use our dominion to bend it to our will. What should be a dominion of love thus becomes one of exploitation and destruction. And so we say, fully—or almost fully—convinced that what we say is true, "This forest does not allow us to do what we wish, therefore let's destroy it. We may be polluting the atmosphere and contributing to global warming, but we need to live more comfortably, to have more goodies, to stimulate the economy." And so on . . .

Evil has so permeated our minds and our wills that its mysterious nature is often used as an excuse not to face and oppose it. We may debate the issues of theodicy for years to come, but the real problem with theodicy is not just that we can come to no satisfactory answer but also that we can use our perplexity as a way not to respond to evil as we should. Admittedly, we cannot explain why an earthquake leaves thousands homeless, but we must not use our puzzlement as a reason not to help them. We do know that homelessness is evil, and we must oppose it. We may debate why climates change, but if such changes lead to failed crops and hunger we are still obliged to combat hunger, which we know is evil. Limited as our understanding may be, we still have a sense of right and wrong. Limited as our power may be, we still are those who have been commanded to till the land and subdue God's creation—to bring it to where it should be. Expelled from Eden—as the "no longer" metaphor puts it—we still must till the earth and tend the present gardens. Awaiting for a better day—as the "not yet" metaphor puts it—we still must work for that better day.

This is what is meant by "stewardship," which cannot be understood without the doctrine of creation and which itself is crucial to a proper understanding of creation and of our role in it. But before we turn to that subject we must consider how it is that God is present in creation, not just at the beginning but even to this day.

Discussion Questions

1. Reread the section of this chapter titled, "The Problem of Evil: Theodicy." What might it mean that evil is real in our world?

2. You may know people who have given up on God or who are angry at God because something bad happened to them. How can you respond? How can you help? Is it OK to be angry with God?

3. For many people, evil is a mystery because we cannot understand how a loving God can allow it. Why do you think bad things happen to good people?

4. How are we to live with the reality of evil? There are different kinds of evil—for example, personal, corporate, systemic. Give examples of each and how you can address them.

5. How can we help people find hope? Where do you see signs of hope in yourself, family, church, community, nation?

God's Presence in Creation

Having come to this point, and fully aware of the power of evil, we might ask, what about the loving parent we met in our first chapter? How is God present in this creation that groans in travail and of which we are part?

Creation Includes Both Nature and History

Throughout history, people have seen the presence of their gods in the world. The Egyptians saw Osiris in the fertilizing floods of the Nile. The Greeks saw Poseidon in the waves of the sea. The Romans saw Diana in the moonlight. And the Aztecs saw Tlaloc in rain and storm. The Hebrews were no exception to this. They too saw Yahweh in the shimmering stars, in the beauty of the rainbow, and in the fertility of the fields. Like Osiris, Poseidon, Diana, and Tlaloc, Yahweh was manifested in nature.

There were, however, two particular notes that made Yahweh different from all these other gods. The first has already been discussed: Yahweh has no equal, no partner, no rival. Yahweh stands alone, not as part of a pantheon or collection of gods but as Creator and ruler of all. Strictly speaking, although the hand of Yahweh may be seen in nature, Yahweh is not a god *of* nature. The second is equally as important: Yahweh is not content with nature and reality as they are but is a god with a purpose, a god who moves nature and society to certain goals. This is what is meant when we say that Yahweh acts not only in nature but also in history. In this context, *history* is not exactly the same as what we studied in school under that name—past events, names, dates, and battles. History is that and much more. History is all that happens within time—in times past, present, and future.

God alone is God.

The very notion of history implies that such happenings are not purely cyclical. There is movement; there is newness. It is this movement, this newness, that distinguishes nature from history. And it is Yahweh's presence and action in that movement that makes Yahweh a god of history—meaning by that not a god who belongs to history but a god who acts in history.

This is not to say that there are no cycles in nature. On the contrary, nature tends to be cyclical. The ancient Egyptians correctly observed that the Nile floods every year to fertilize the land—or at least it did until the building of the Aswan dam—and attributed that to the death and rising of Osiris. Today we know that the flooding of the Nile is due to the annual rainy season much farther south. Although these two explanations are radically different, both agree in explaining the cycle of floods by means of other cycles—in one case, the annual rising of Osiris, and in the other the annual rains in central Africa. Some Amerindians in Mesoamerica believed that the cyclical setting of the sun, and its cyclical waning and waxing with the passing of the seasons, had to do with the sun being fatigued and requiring nourishment—sometimes even nourishment in the form of human blood. Today we know that these phenomena have to do with the rotation of earth and the inclination of its axis as it follows its orbit around the sun. The two explanations are very different but both still refer to cyclical occurrences—in the case of modern astronomy, the cycles of earth's rotation on its own axis and the cycles of its orbit around the sun.

In the ancient world, the observation of the cycles of the moon, which could be divided by four to make cycles of seven, led to the notion of a seven-day week. It was on the basis of that seven-day cycle that most of the Near East developed its calendar. This may be seen also in the Hebrew calendar as well as in the Hebrew scriptures where number seven is a sign of perfection as well as the basis for other cycles. A week of weeks after Passover, that is, forty-nine days, comes the fiftieth day, or Pentecost. Number seven rules not only the days of the week but also the counting of years. Thus, every seventh year, at the end of a week of years, would be a sabbatical year. And after every week of weeks of years—that is, after forty-nine years, would come the Year of Jubilee.

But the Hebrews were not content with such cycles. Cycles, by their very nature, are repetitive. In themselves, they lead nowhere—as we acknowledge in the common phrase, "going around in circles." The Hebrews, while acknowledging the cycles of nature, also believed that Yahweh was leading creation somewhere. God was doing something new. Hence the announcement of the prophets, "Behold, I am doing something new." (See Isa 43:19; Jer 31:22; Rev 21:5.)

Significantly, while the Hebrews did adopt and adapt the feasts of neighboring peoples celebrating crops and other such annual occurrences, their great feasts celebrated particular events in which God had moved history forward. Of these the greatest was Passover, which commemorated the day in which the angel of the Lord killed the firstborn among the Egyptians but passed over the homes of the children of Israel, which were marked as such with the blood of the sacrificial lamb.

Patterns in History

But the Hebrews also believed that Yahweh is not a capricious God. Yahweh does not act one way today and another tomorrow. This means that, although history is not cyclical, there are in it patterns that repeat themselves. The very pattern of Passover, where God opens the sea so that the people may move to freedom, is repeated in the return from exile, where prophets speak of God making a road in the desert just as earlier God had made a road in the sea. Significantly, when centuries later Mark the evangelist wrote of John the Baptist, he presented him after the pattern of the exilic prophet announcing God's liberating action—"*a voice shouting out in the wilderness*" (Mark 1:3). Like the prophets of old, John would announce a return from exile into a land of promise, an opening of the sea into a promise of freedom.

Another such pattern presents God as choosing the small and the apparently insignificant in order to achieve great things. God chooses an elderly couple, Abraham and Sarah, to be the progenitors of a great nation. God chooses Joseph, sold as a slave, to rule Egypt and save his family from starvation. God chooses a boy cast adrift on the river to be the great liberator and the lawgiver of Israel. God chooses the barren Hannah to be the mother of the great prophet Samuel. God chooses David, the smallest in all his brood, to be the great king. God chooses the "little town of Bethlehem" to be the birthplace of the Messiah. And this pattern continues in the New Testament where God chooses the stone that was rejected by the builders to be the cornerstone of the entire edifice.

There is another such pattern that is particularly noteworthy for us here: although obviously God is present everywhere and may be seen and worshipped everywhere, God chooses particular places to be manifest and to be available to the people—available in a way that is both loving and majestic. God speaks to Noah in the rainbow and to Moses in the burning bush. God dwells in the ark of the covenant and then in the temple. And then, in the New Testament, God is in Jesus, in whom "all the fullness of God was pleased to dwell" (Col 1:19 NRSV). This is a theme that many ancient Christian writers embraced, speaking of Jesus as "the temple" in which God dwells. Unfortunately, this has sometimes been interpreted as creating a gulf between humanity and divinity in Jesus, while in fact the Old Testament image of God dwelling in the temple was intended to lead in the opposite direction. Just as God is particularly present in the temple, and must be worshipped with particular devotion in the temple, so is the divinity closely and indissoluble bound with the humanity of Jesus—but this is a subject for another book!

God's actions in history follow a pattern of love and redemption.

Finally, God's actions in history follow a pattern of love and redemption. Ancient Christian writers pointed out that immediately after expelling the first couple from Eden God provided them with furs, a more suitable cover than the leaves they were wearing. Furthermore, God expelled them from the garden not because God no longer loved them but because were they to eat of the tree of life they would live forever, and this would be a wretched fate in their state of sin and disobedience. Thus, in a way even death is an act of God's mercy—which is why St. Francis could sing to "Sister Death."

All of these patterns—and many others—show God's constant love for creation, specifically for humankind, and may be seen in the history of Israel, of the church, and of the world. Ancient Christian writers called these patterns "types" or "figures" and read them as pointing to their culmination, first in Jesus and then in the final reign of God. For this reason, this sort of biblical interpretation is called "typology."

While all this may seem far-fetched to a modern reader, when we take the time to consider it there is much to be said for it. Even without acknowledging it, when we study and teach history in our schools we are doing so because, consciously or not, we believe that there are patterns in human history and that knowing these patterns may be of help as we face present and future decisions. Interesting as they may be, we do not study the rise and decline of the Roman Empire, or the French Revolution, or Lincoln's presidency, or the Great Depression out of mere curiosity. We study them because we believe they may teach us something useful for the times in which we live.

The Workings of History

This means that, by its very nature, the very concept of history requires both newness on the one hand and recurring patterns on the other. This is the way the entire Judeo-Christian tradition looks at history. History is not cyclical. It never repeats itself. But history is not a mere line, always moving into something new with no reference to the past, always surprising and capricious. Every day is different; and yet, every day the sun rises in the east and sets in the west. Thus, if we seek a geometric figure to depict the nature of history, a spiral would be better than either a circle or a straight line. History moves. History does not repeat itself. And yet, past events in history provide us wisdom and experience with which to face present events and plan for the future. And, let it be said in passing, this understanding of history is one of the reasons why the Judeo-Christian world has embraced the notions of newness and progress that have led to the theory of evolution, on the one hand, and to astounding technological development— good and bad—on the other. Such development is always based in knowledge acquired by others in the past and now amplified and applied in a different way.

Patterns of God's Presence in Creation

If we then return to our theme of creation, and consider God's presence and action in it, all the patterns mentioned above become significant.

The first of those patterns already mentioned is that God chooses and uses the small and the apparently insignificant in order to achieve great things. As pointed out above, this may be seen throughout biblical history. Its culmination is in Jesus, the stone that the expert builders rejected, but God has made the cornerstone of a new creation. Some scholars speak of this theme in the Gospels—particularly in Luke—as "the great reversal": the last shall be first, the kingdom will not belong to the empire builders but to the peacemakers, those who are hungry shall be filled, those who are now full will go away empty...

Paul tells the Corinthians—and us—that this pattern continues in the life of the church:

> Where are the wise? Where are the legal experts? Where are today's debaters? Hasn't God made the wisdom of the world foolish?...
>
> Look at your situation when you were called, brothers and sisters! By ordinary human standards not many were wise, not many were powerful, not many were from the upper class. But God chose what the world considers foolish to shame the wise. God chose what the world considers weak to shame the strong. And God chose what the world considers low-class and low-life—what is considered to be nothing—to reduce what is considered to be something to nothing. (1 Cor 1:20, 26-28)

Martin Luther affirmed the same, declaring that the best way to know God is not in glory, power, wisdom, or majesty. Instead of such a "theology of glory," he proposes a "theology of the cross," in which one seeks and sees God not in glory and wisdom but in the weakness, suffering, and folly of the cross.

On this basis, one may well say that the most important events in human history, those that move history toward its intended goal, are not the earth-shaking, first-page news items but millions of lesser, less noticeable events of justice, peace, and love. Granted, this is something that the eyes cannot see nor the mind fathom. But it reflects the equally invisible and unfathomable victory of Christ through suffering and death.

God chooses unlikely people in surprising, unexpected places.

The second pattern is of a piece with the first: God choosing to dwell in particular and unexpected places—a box carried by nomads in the desert, a temple in the capital of a fourth-rate power. Christians hold that all those places are "types" of "figures" pointing to the supreme instance of divine presence among us: Jesus of Nazareth, the Christ. God is present everywhere, yes. But God is particularly present in Jesus Christ. And Jesus himself is present everywhere, but he has given us two particular places where we may meet him. The first is the communion of the church, the body of Christ, where in breaking bread together we discern that we, this motley crowd out of every tribe and nation, are the place where both we ourselves and others are invited to meet God. The second is even more surprising. According to Jesus himself, we meet, feed, and clothe him in the hungry and the naked. Talk about a great reversal! God is present in history. We can meet God in history. God is readily available to us. Yet this is not primarily in the palaces and seats of power but in the cardboard shacks of the homeless; it is not primarily in the banquets of the rich and famous but in a meal in which all sorts of people break bread together.

The third pattern is that God's love never fails, even though we may not see it. In the Genesis story, the first couple was probably not too happy being exiled from Eden, but this was an act of God's love. As we shall see in the next chapter, even when we do not see that hand of God, God still loves us. God loves all of creation—all of this wayward and rebellious creation.

> God's love never fails. God's presence abides with us forever.

God's Strange Rule

Over sixty years ago, I had a professor whose favorite words were, "God writes straight with our crooked human lines." By this he meant that God has given us the freedom to make bad decisions, to turn in the wrong direction. God does not force us to do what is right. But in some mysterious ways, even using our crooked lines, God leads history to God's intended ends.

This may be seen repeatedly in the biblical narrative. Joseph's brothers sold him into slavery with no good intention whatsoever. They simply hated him and wanted to be rid of him. But in the end, when Joseph is a ruler in Egypt and is thus able to save his family from starvation, Joseph himself sees the hand of God working through his brothers' treachery. In other words, their lines were crooked, but even with them God wrote straight. And, if we look at the entire narrative, we see that there are in it other crooked lines—for instance, the false accusations of Potiphar's wife that land Joseph in prison and whatever Pharaoh's chief baker and chief cupbearer did, or were suspected of doing, that put them in prison with Joseph. With the crooked lines of Joseph's brother and of Potiphar's wife God wrote the straight line of Joseph's being able to save his brothers. Yet we may well imagine that Joseph was not too happy when he was sold into slavery or when he was imprisoned in punishment for something he had not done.

This too may be seen as a pattern or "type" of God's action, for similar factors appear in the story of Jesus. God wrote straight with the crooked lines of Herod, Judas, Caiaphas, and Pilate. Yet even Jesus, being who he was, was not happy as these things were taking place. In the garden of Gethsemane he prayed, "My Father, if it's possible, take this cup of suffering away from me" (Matt 26:39). And from the cross he protested, "My God, my God, why have you left me?" (Matt 27:46).

Which means that protesting, questioning the acts of God, is not an act of unbelief as is often thought. We question God and we protest against God because we know that God is there. We know that God is powerful. We know that God is loving. And yet somehow this loving and powerful God seems to have abandoned us. And thus we protest like Jesus, "My God, my God, why have you left me?" or like the psalmist, "My God, I cry out during the day, / but you don't answer; / even at nighttime I don't stop" (Ps 22:2).

God is present in creation. But God is neither a spectator nor a puppeteer. A spectator would simply let things happen, no matter where they may lead. Such is not God's way. God does "pull strings" to make things happen—saving Moses from Pharaoh, and Jesus from Herod, choosing the elderly Abraham and Sarah, and the exceedingly young David. But in pulling strings a puppeteer runs the entire show in which the puppets really have no say. This also is not God's way. As we have seen, it is out of love that God has given human creatures free will—a free will that we will most likely misuse. And God respects that freedom.

> ## Joseph to his brothers: "You planned something bad for me, but God produced something good from it" (Gen 50:20).

How are we to understand that? How are we to reconcile our faith in a loving and powerful God with our perplexity and our suffering? One way is to look at a metaphor that is fully biblical but we have often ignored or taken to be a sign of unbelief. This metaphor is the absence of God.

Discussion Questions

1. Where do you see new things happening? How are younger generations different from older generations? Share the last new big-ticket item that you bought and/or describe the newest member of your family.

2. Who are persons in the Bible that God chose? Often God chooses the small and the apparently insignificant in order to achieve great things. Remember and talk about the stories of David, Joseph, Rachel, Abraham, and Sarah.

3. God's actions in history follow a pattern of love and redemption. Share a time when someone you know was lost but now is found. What are some ways that God reaches out to people today? How does your church reach out in love to new members, visitors, and strangers?

4. We participate in God's gift of love when we share our time, talents, gifts, service, and witness with those in need. Perhaps that is why God loves a cheerful giver. How do you share your time, talents, gifts, service, and witness with others at home, at church, at work, in your community?

God's Absence from Creation

A God Who Rests

At the end of chapter 1, we saw that ours is a God who rests. This means that God is not always available to us at our beck and call. There is much Christian preaching that ignores this. We are told that if we want something, all we have to do is pray, and if we have enough faith God will give it to us. This denies and undercuts the sovereignty of God. God is not like a drink-dispensing machine: you put in your coins, and out comes the drink. Such a god is in truth an idol, a god constantly and continually at our disposal, ready to do our bidding.

No. Our God is a God who rests, a God who is not always available. In the Genesis story, God is not right there to tell the man and the woman not to fall to the wiles of the serpent. God plants the garden, creates the human couple, gives them some directions, and then seems to leave them to their own devices. This means that in a sense God forsakes creation; God leaves creatures to fend for themselves. Although often forgotten, this is a fundamental aspect of the faith of Israel. Thus, the psalmist cries,

> Just like a deer that craves streams of water,
>   my whole beings craves you, God.
> My whole being thirsts for God, for the living God.
>   When will I come and see God's face?
> My tears have been my food both day and night,
>   as people constantly questioned me,
>   "Where's your God now?"
> . . . .
> I say to God, my solid rock,
>   "Why have you forgotten me?
>   Why do I have to walk around,
>   sad, oppressed by enemies?"
> With my bones crushed, my foes make fun of me,
>   constantly questioning me: "Where's your God now?"
>   (Ps 42:1-3, 9-10)

And in that other psalm quoted at the end of the previous chapter:

> My God! my God,
>   why have you left me all alone?
>   Why are you so far from saving me—
>   so far from my anguished groans?
> My God, I cry out during the day,
>   but you don't answer;
>   even at night I don't stop. (Ps 22:1-2)

And in another:

> Wake up! Why are you sleeping, Lord?
>> Get up! Don't reject us forever!
> Why are you hiding your face,
>> forgetting our suffering and oppression?
> Look: we're going down to the dust;
>> our stomachs are flat to the ground.
> Stand up! Help us!
>> Save us for the sake of your faithful love. (Ps 44:23-26)

Lest we think that such complaints are the result of a lack of faith, it is important to point out that in each of these psalms there remains an unshakable faith in God's power and God's love. Thus, the psalmist who thirsts after God and who feels pressed by those who constantly ask, "Where is your God?" can still say,

> Why, I ask myself, are you so depressed?
>> Why are you so upset inside?
>>> Hope in God!
>>> Because I will again give him thanks,
>>> my saving grace and my God. (Ps 42:11)

The psalmist who complains that God has forsaken him, that God will not answer his prayers either by day or by night, can still declare,

> Every part of the earth
>> will remember and come back to the Lord;
>> every family among all the nations will worship you.
> Because the right to rule belongs to the LORD,
>> he rules all nations.

Indeed, all the earth's powerful
> will worship him;
> all who are descending to the dust
> will kneel before him;
> my being also lives for him. (Ps 22:27-29)

Finally, the one who tries to waken God from slumber does not forget that

we have heard it, God, with our own ears;
> our ancestors told us about it:
>> about the deeds you did in their days,
>> in days long past. (Ps 44:1)

What we have in all these psalms—and in many other places in scripture—is the complaint that God is at rest; God is not like a Coke machine ready to dispense solace whenever we put our coins in the slot. In all of these laments, the psalmist wishes that God were always actively manifesting God's power but ultimately recognizes that God's power is such that it does not have to be proven at every turn. God's power is not manifested only in the act of creation; it is manifested also in the fact that creation still functions when God rests. In short, God's power and love are manifested not only in God's presence but also in God's apparent absence.

Like children learn about their parents, we must learn that God is present even when we don't see God.

An Absent God

Even though we seldom note it, the theme of the absence of God is central to the teachings of Jesus. In some of the parables, it is we who are absent from God. The lost sheep has to be found. The lost coin has to be found. The prodigal has to return. But in other parables it would seem that the issue is not our absence from God but rather God's absence from us. We call these stories "parables of stewardship." And this is an excellent name for them, for stewardship is precisely what a steward practices when the master is away. While the master is there, a steward's role is limited. It is when the master is away that the steward must take responsibility. In one of his best known parables (Matt 25:14-30), Jesus tells of a man who, "leaving on a trip," called three of his servants, gave to each a large amount of money (five talents to one, two to another, and one to a third) and "then he left." In other words, the parable is about how to manage while the Master is not present. Similarly, the parallel parable in Luke 19:12-27—the parable of the ten pounds— begins with the words, "A certain man who was born into royalty went to a distant land..."—in other words, he absented himself. In another parable in the same twenty-fifth chapter of Matthew where we find the parable of the talents, Jesus speaks of ten bridesmaids going out to seek the bridegroom. But the bridegroom is delayed—that is to say, he is not present at the time when they expected him to be.

In Matthew 21 Jesus tells another parable of absence: "There was a landowner who planted a vineyard. He put a fence around it, dug a winepress in it, and built a tower. Then he rented it to tenant farmers and took a trip" (v. 33). There is a clear parallelism between this parable and the story of creation.

God made the earth and all that is in it, and planted a garden, and gave it to the human couple to till. And it was all very good. And then God rested!

There are many other parables of absence in the teachings of Jesus. A master returns and discovers how a servant has been keeping his household. A thief comes at night when people least expect him.

We often speak of the presence of God, and rightly so. But this other theme or metaphor of absence is also common in the Bible. Even apart from sin, God gives the human creature space, freedom to exercise its responsibility. As we have seen, in the story in the garden, after creating humans and giving them dominion over the rest of creation, God lets them exercise that dominion, even though it also implies the possibility of sin. And this absence, just as much as the divine presence, is a sign of love.

Absence as an Act of Love

In chapter 1 we spoke of creation as an expression of God's love as a parent. Now we must look likewise at God's rest, at God's apparent absence. The point in chapter 1 was that, just as earthly parents deciding to have a child are also deciding to create something beyond themselves, not entirely in their control, so God's decision to create the world and to create us is a decision to create something beyond Godself, and not entirely under God's control—even though we know that ultimately God's purposes shall prevail.

Now the image of parenthood may be taken one step further. Parental love is not manifested only in the act of procreation, and not only in the many actions of feeding, nurturing, and guiding, but also in a parent's acts of absence. Out of love a parent finds it necessary to step back and let a child try its wings, even at the risk of pain and failure. A parent who is always present, guarding a child from every risk and every hurt, is not a very good parent. A child whose parents are always hovering around, guarding the child's every step, will never learn to walk. And a child who is never given the responsibility of making decisions, even at the risk of error, will never grow up. Out of love, a parent must step back. Likewise, God's parental love is manifested not only in creation and in sustenance but also in God's apparent absence—in God's letting us run our lives and much of the world by ourselves, even at the risk of ruining both.

Søren Kierkegaard expresses this more fully in his book *Gospel of Sufferings*:

> When a child is allowed to hold on to his mother's dress, can we say then he is walking along with her, just as his mother walks? Nay, we may not say so. First must the child learn to walk alone and on his own, before he can go the way his mother goes, and go as she is going. And when the child is learning to walk alone, what must the mother do? She must make herself invisible. That her tenderness towards him is the same and remains unaltered, that indeed it probably grows greater, just at the time when the child is learning to walk alone, we know very well; the child, on the other hand, may not always understand it. But what is meant by the child having to learn to walk alone and to walk on his own is, in a spiritual sense, the task set anyone who is to be somebody's follower—he must learn to walk alone and to walk on his own. Strange, is it not? . . . That heaven's care for us in unchanged, and is indeed, were it possible, still more

solicitous in this hour of danger, we know very well, but perhaps we cannot always understand it, when we are learning.[1]

And Julian of Norwich expresses it similarly. She writes,

The mother may sometimes suffer the child to fall and to be distressed in various ways, for its own benefit.... And if we do not feel ourselves eased, let us at once be sure that he is behaving as a wise Mother. For if he sees that it is profitable to us to mourn and to weep, with compassion and pity he suffers us until the right time has come, out of his love.[2]

We are learning. We are learning to live as God's children in a world where the hand of our eternal parent is not always visible, in a world where God has placed us to be stewards of the absent master, to grow as we could not were God always holding our hand and guiding our every step. We are intended to grow after the likeness of our parent, and in our parent's name to have dominion over creation.

One thing, however, is certain: stewardship is not ownership. In the ancient world, a steward was often a trusted slave and thus part of the owner's property. He was above the rest of the household, but he was still part of the household. The doctrine of creation tells us that this is a perfect illustration of the human role and condition. We are creatures, and as such are part of creation; but we are also God's stewards, and as such have been given dominion over creation.

Stewards in the Midst of Evil

Sadly, the divine absence has an added dimension, for sin has come into the picture. This is indeed God's world. But it is God's rebellious world. This world, made by God, is also godless. It is a world of injustice and oppression, of war and prejudice, of hate and falsehood. In this godless world of God, the image that appears so frequently in the parables, of the absence of the master, is both a realistic description of our present situation and a call to responsibility. While the master is away, the steward must run things according to the will of the absent master. The steward cannot consult the master at every move, for the steward must learn the master's mind, and this can only be done if the master is not constantly supervising, constantly telling the steward what to do. There are times when we do not hear a clear word from God. It is precisely at those times that it is most important to know the master's mind; and, paradoxically, it may be precisely at those times that we grow closer to God—just as a child grows closer to her mother when she learns to walk on her own, when she has to make decisions on her own, when she has children of her own.

Our task is to learn the master's mind and know the master's heart.

Learning the master's mind: that is a steward's primary task. To this the steward must devote every effort, both when the master is present and when the master is not. When the master is present and speaks, a good steward heeds the voice of the master and takes note. When the master is absent or silent, a good steward takes the risk of acting on the basis of what is known of the master's mind, knowing full well that it is quite possible that the master will find fault in what the steward did.

In such cases it is better to take a risk, as the managers of five and of two talents did, than to "play it safe," as their counterpart with one talent did. Like a loving parent, this master of ours wishes for us to grow, and every parent knows that there is no growth without risk.

But even so, the sometimes absent master has given us much whereby to learn the master's mind. In a way, this is the function of scripture; this is the function of the community of believers; this is the function of conscience. Yet none of these—not even all three together—are a guarantee of divine approval. The risk is still there. The talents must still be invested in a market that is always uncertain. Faithful Christians do not all agree on every course of action. A steward's decisions are not always easy. God's absence is often compounded by God's silence. Not only do we not see the hand of God, we also do not hear God's voice. At that point, we find ourselves in the precarious position of a steward whose master is absent and who must make a difficult decision without having received direct instructions. As God's stewards of creation, we each and all must take the risk of acting according to what we believe to be God's will—like a faithful steward who makes a decision hoping that this is what the master would wish him to do. Along that path, we must support, encourage, and forgive one another as we all seek to discover and do God's will.

But such support does not eliminate the uncertainty and precariousness of our actions and decisions as God's stewards. We often find ourselves questioning: "Lord, have I done the right thing? Was there a better course of action? Have I done enough? Have I done too much? How will my action affect others, both now and in future generations? Please, Lord, set my mind at ease!"

It is not surprising that such questioning often leads to anguish, and anguish leads to despair, and despair leads to inaction, and inaction leads back to further anguish.... And we are trapped in a cycle that becomes an eddy that threatens to drown us and prevents us from being the stewards we are called to be.

This is because we forget that God's creative act is not only an act of love but also an act of hope. To this we shall turn in our last chapter.

Discussions Questions

1. What does it mean that God rests? Do you get adequate rest, vacation time, time off from your responsibilities? How could you help give someone else the opportunity to find peace and rest?

2. If creation is an expression of God's love as a parent, what signs of love do you see in creation?

3. Giving children supervision is a parent's responsibility, but how much is too much or too little?

4. Do you do better when you are closely supervised or when you are not? Who is supervising you? What makes for a good supervisor?

5. When God is perceived as absent, we in the church must step forward. What are ways that your church can be God's hands and feet in the world and your neighborhood?

6. How do you teach a child to be obedient? What does it mean to be "[freed] for joyful obedience"[3] (see 1 John 5)?

Creation and Hope

We have already seen that a parent's greatest act of love is deciding to have a child, even while knowing that this child will not always be obedient and will probably cause the parent much heartbreak. The parent does this not only out of love but also out of hope. Even knowing that there may be difficult times ahead, a good parent decides to have this child in the hope that even through those difficult times, and certainly at the end, the child will become a mature and responsible human being.

God's loving act of creation is also an act of hope. In creating and sustaining the world and humankind, God hopes that they will become what they are not. And, because God is who God is, this hope is also a promise, and this promise is also a certainly!

There is a revealing passage in Paul's letter to the Romans in which he speaks of the future of creation:

> I believe that the present suffering is nothing compared to the coming glory that is going to be revealed to us. The whole creation waits breathless with anticipation for the revelation of God's sons and daughters. Creation was subjected to frustration, not by its own choice—it was the choice of

the one who subjected it—but in the hope that the creation itself will be set free from slavery to decay and bought into the glorious freedom of God's children. We know that the whole creation is groaning together and suffering labor pains up until now. And it's not only the creation. We ourselves who have the Spirit as the first crop of the harvest also groan inside as we wait to be adopted and for our bodies to be set free. (Rom 8:18-23)

In order to understand this passage it is important to note, first of all, that Paul is not trying to explain or to understand evil—which, as we saw earlier, is impossible to do. In the verses immediately preceding, Paul is dealing rather with the condition of believers and their suffering. His response is that, while at times we may not see it, we are in fact "God's children. But if we are children, we are also heirs. We are God's heirs and fellow heirs with Christ" (Rom 8:16b-17a).

As children of God, we have the privilege of a relationship with God.

The very notion of being an heir is a sign of a future condition, and this is what Paul is stressing in the entire passage. Being an heir of God means that we have the certain promise that we are not yet all we shall be—that what we shall be is not readily visible. But being an heir is not only a matter of the future; it is also a matter of a present relationship. Our adoption as children of God points to the future, but it also impacts the present and how we view ourselves. For this reason, many in the early church objected to kneeling in prayer on Sundays because this is the day of the resurrection, of our adoption as heirs. A prince does not approach a king who is also a loving father by kneeling or groveling but by looking face to face, with the absolute certainty of the king's love and faithfulness.

On a similar vein, Paul is telling the Romans that their true being has not yet come to fruition. In Colossians he tells his readers that "you died, and your life is hidden with Christ in God. When Christ, who is your life, is revealed, then you also will be revealed with him in glory" (Col 3:3-4). In other words, something has changed, but this is a sign of a greater and glorious change.

In the passage from Romans quoted earlier, most interpreters agree that "the one who subjected it" is God. But this is not a subjection of oppression. It is not that God decided to subject creation so that it would forever be God's slave. On the contrary, it is a subjection in hope, much as when a truly loving parent subjects a child not out of a desire to be obeyed and to rule the child's life but rather out of a vision of what the child is to become—out of the same loving hope that was there even before the child was conceived. God has not subjected creation as a master subjects a slave but rather as a loving parent subjects a child. This means that, like a child, creation is not yet what it will be. Like a child, it is going through growing pains, but these pains lead to a future maturity of love, peace, and justice.

It is not only Paul who announces such a glowing future. The Bible abounds in visions and metaphoric descriptions of that future. Among these are the vision of the peaceable kingdom in Isaiah 11:6-9; the promise in Micah of a day when "they will beat their swords into iron plows," and when "they will sit underneath their own grapevines, under their own fig trees. / There will be no one to terrify them (Mic 4:3b-4a); and the heavenly city in Revelation 21:9-27. Clearly, all of these are metaphors. We really have very little idea of the future that God has prepared for this creation—and for us. We do not know how the enmity between the lion and the lamb, or among nations, can be overcome, nor what such a world would be like. We do not really expect a huge city, several miles wide, several miles long, and several miles tall. But we do expect the peace, joy, and justice to which these images point.

God created us in hope and in expectation for what we can become.

Back to Paul's words in Romans: here Paul uses the imagery of parenting, which we have encountered throughout this book. However, now the reference is not to God as a parent, but rather to the whole of creation as a mother about to give birth. Carrying a child is no easy task for a mother, and even that is almost like nothing compared to the pains of labor itself—what Paul calls the "suffering labor pains" (Rom 8:22). Yet those pains are followed by rejoicing in the child itself. And that joy is such that it cannot be compared with the groans of pain that preceded it.

Then Paul extends the image further: it is not only creation that is groaning in travail awaiting the birth of the new creation but also we who "have the Spirit as the first crop of the harvest" are still groaning as in travail as we await "to be adopted and for our bodies to be set free," the day when our adoption as God's children will be made manifest—or, as Colossians would put it, the day when our life, which is now hidden in Christ, will be revealed.

When properly made, the decision to have a child is both a sign of love and a sign of hope—love for the child who will certainly disobey the parents, and hope for what that child will become through a process of maturing. Likewise, God's act of creation is a sign of both love and hope—love for creatures that will go astray, and hope for the future of creation, the glorious future that will come after all the groans and pains of travail.

Hope, however, is too weak a word to express the nature of this expectation. In our common usage, *hope* has a wide range of meanings. If I say, "I hope you did as you promised," what I actually mean is that I do not quite trust you and your promise. If I say, "I hope it doesn't rain on our picnic next week," what I am expressing is hardly more than a wish. If I say, "I hope to become a pastor someday," I am saying that this is a goal toward which I am striving. Yet none of these even approaches what Christian hope really is—the hope of which Paul speaks in Romans.

Christian hope surpasses all other hopes because is in not simply an expression of something we would like to see happen—like having sunshine for a picnic—nor even of something toward which we strive—like becoming a pastor. It is the firm knowledge that God's power is such that we can rest in the knowledge that, despite the rebelliousness of creation, ultimately the future is in the hands of God, and God's love is such that we know that whatever that future might be it will be one of love.

The God who has made—and continues making and sustaining—all things out of love is the same God who out of the same love will bring all things to their intended end. Meanwhile, we live by faith in that God of love and by hope and expectation of what that God will bring about.

Creation—all of creation, including ourselves—is the apple of God's eye. It is the result of God's love, and it is the object of God's love. It is the result and the object of that "love divine, all loves excelling," of this "joy of heaven, to earth come down" to which Charles Wesley sang.[1] It is to this that the doctrine of creation points: to God's love for all and for all things—to God's love at the beginning, to God's love now, to God's love at the end!

Discussion Questions

1. What does it mean to be your parents' child? What advantages and disadvantages did you receive by virtue of them being your parents? How are you like and unlike your parents? How are your children like and unlike you?

2. What is the difference between being God's child and God's servant? What are our responsibilities as God's children to God?

3. Who is the apple of your eye? What does it mean to you that you are the apple of God's eye?

4. What gives you joy? How do you share it?

5. As God's people, we are children of the light. What does that play out in your everyday life?

Notes

2. Creation as an Act of Love

1. Martin Buber, *I and Thou* (New York: Charles Scribner's Sons, 1958), 14–15.

2. Lionel S. Thurston, quoted in Claude Welch, *In This Name: The Doctrine of the Trinity in Contemporary Theology* (New York: Charles Scribner's Sons, 1952), 136–37.

3. Leonardo Boff, *Holy Trinity, Perfect Communion* (Maryknoll, NY: Orbis Books, 2000), 3. Originally published in Portuguese in 1988.

3. The Human Creature

1. Gregory of Nyssa, *On the Making of Man* 2 in *A Select Library of Nicene and Post-Nicene Fathers of the Christian Church*, ed. Philip Schaff and Henry Wace, reprint (Grand Rapids: Wm. B. Eerdmans, n.d.), 5:390.

2. Irenaus, *Irenaeus against Heresies* 5.16.2 in *The Ante-Nicene Fathers*, ed. Alexander Roberts and James Donaldson, reprint (Grand Rapids: Eerdmans, 1956), 1:544.

3. Thomas Aquinas, *Summa theologica* 3, q. 1, art. 3. Author's translation.

4. Pierre Teilhard de Chardin, *The Phenomenon of Man* (New York: Harper & Row, 1959), 258.

5. Gregory of Nyssa, *Homily 4 on Ecclesiastes*, Migne, *Patrologia Graeca*, 44:435.

6. Vine Deloria, *God Is Red: A Native View of Religion* (New York: Grosset & Dunlap, 1973), 96.

7. Terence E. Fretheim, "Genesis," *The New Interpreter's Bible* (Nashville: Abingdon, 1994), 1:346.

8. Reinhold Niebuhr, *The Nature and Destiny of Man: A Christian Interpretation* (New York: Charles Scribner's Sons, 1955), 1:3.

9. Ibid., 1:4.

4. Enter Evil

1. J. L. Mackie, "Evil and Omnipotence," in *God and Evil*, ed. Nelson Pike (Englewood Cliffs, NJ: Prentice Hall, 1964), 47–48.

6. God's Absence from Creation

1. Søren Kierkegaard, *Gospel of Sufferings*, trans. A. S. Aldworth and W. S. Ferrie (London: James Clarke, 1955), 15–16.

2. Julian of Norwich, *Showings* (New York: Paulist Press, 1978), 300–1.

3. *The United Methodist Hymnal* (Nashville: The United Methodist Publishing House, 1989), 8.

7. Creation and Hope

1. "Love Divine, All Loves Excelling," *The United Methodist Hymnal* (Nashville: The United Methodist Publishing House, 1989), 384.

CPSIA information can be obtained at www.ICGtesting.com
Printed in the USA
LVOW11s0600180915

454622LV00003B/3/P